David Morris

FIGHTING BACK

Recovering from a near-fatal stroke
to find a new life in the sun

Mereo Books

Mereo Books 2nd Floor, 6-8 Dyer Street,
Cirencester, Gloucestershire, GL7 2PF

An imprint of Memoirs Book Ltd. www.mereobooks.com

Fighting Back: 978-1-86151-941-2

First published in Great Britain in 2019
by Mereo Books, an imprint of Memoirs Books Ltd.

The address for Memoirs Books Ltd. can be
found at www.memoirspublishing.com

Memoirs Books Ltd. Reg. No. 7834348

Typeset in 10/17pt Century Schoolbook
by Wiltshire Associates Ltd.
Printed and bound in Great Britain

Contents

PREFACE

This book is a true account, my story in my words, of what happened to me following a near-fatal stroke at the age of only 48. It explains why a stroke doesn't have to be the end of your life but the beginning of a new one, though a very different one. I want this book to be an inspiration to anyone who suffers a stroke, or in fact any life-changing happening. Yes, bad things can happen in our lives, but it's how we deal with them that counts. Don't throw in the towel, it's too easy to give up – fight back! Human life is so very fragile and so short. Bad things happen in our lives, but they can make us stronger.

It's a wonderful world we have around us, but sometimes it is forgotten or lost.

* * *

Whenever you find yourself doubting how far you can go
Just remember how far you have come.
Remember everything you have faced,
All the battles you have won
And all the fears you have overcome.

Chapter 1

The bomb goes off

Apart from having a hangover from hell, going to bed on the night of Wednesday September 18 2013 seemed no different from any other night. But what was to happen the following morning would change my life forever, and I'm still not sure why.

I remember the alarm going off; it had been set for 7 am. I was due at work on what we called the late shift for the Newcastle branch of John Lewis in Eldon Square, starting at 11 am and finishing at 8 pm, when the store closed. We had three shifts in the area I worked in, with a team of four, the early shift, from 6.30 am to 3.30 pm, a daylight shift from 9 am to 6 and the late shift from 11 to 8. These shifts not only covered the shop opening hours but the hours needed to operate our customer collection system. I was up at 7 as always for the late shift, as I liked a bit of time to myself before starting work, whatever shift I was on. I would walk to work and home again, whatever the weather, and had done this all my working life; I had been at John Lewis since 1981, and had never been late for work.

I had worked at two branches of John Lewis, starting at Jessop & Son in my home city of Nottingham on July 7 1981 until I moved up north to Newcastle, getting a branch transfer to John Lewis Newcastle, formerly known as Bainbridge's. Then I did something stupid – I got married. I never thought I would get married, and if I'm honest all this had happened far too quickly. I never felt part of my family with my wife and her two sons. This was in 2005. The marriage lasted eight years until my wife developed BSE – bovine spongiform encephalopathy, or mad cow disease. Things got too much and I moved out of the marital home and was living in a shared house at 66 Brighton Grove in the Fenham area of Newcastle.

When I stepped out of bed that Thursday morning, I remember falling on the floor, but could not work out why. I tried to get up, but was unable to do so. My only concern at the time was the noise I had made, and not wanting to trouble Eduardo, who lived in flat 1 below me. Again I tried to get up, but I could not lift myself off the floor. I couldn't understand it. My last thought before I passed out was that I had to get up and get to work, as in 32 years I had never been late and had very rarely had time off sick, something on which I prided myself.

My next recollection was that the police, a paramedic and my wife Gail were standing over me in my room. It is all vague, but I remember the black and green uniforms and my wife coming into my room and finding me on the floor where I had fallen. They had got a key from my letting agent, as it was now Saturday lunchtime. I had been missing from work for two and a half days! My employers, my wife and everyone had been trying to contact me on my mobile phone, but I had been unable to answer as I must have passed out until I was awoken by these three intruders.

The police and paramedic started to ask me a series of questions. It must have been a procedure they have. It all seemed a bit hazy, much like a bad dream, but I can remember the questions:

'What is your name?'

'Where do you live?'

'How old are you and when is your birthday?'

Of course I answered all the questions correctly.

'What day is it?'

'Thursday,' I replied.

'No, it's Saturday lunchtime' said one of the emergency services people.

'It can't be,' I said.

'You've been missing,' said Gail. They all assured me it was Saturday. I had been absent from work for the previous two days, and with no news from me they knew something was wrong and had telephoned my wife, again a procedure they had in place for situations like this. The first number on my list was Gail's, and then the police had been contacted. But how could Thursday have turned into Saturday? I had no recollection of day turning into night or night turning into day. I must have passed out after falling, and I was now in a very bad way. The paramedics had got to me just in time, as my body was beginning to shut down. I was severely dehydrated, with no food or water for nearly three days. The paramedics told me that within a couple of hours my body would have begun to shut down and I would have been a goner.

All my main organs were a mess. My liver and kidneys were failing, and my heart was beating so fast that was at risk of a heart attack. Human life is so fragile. I had been close to death, but it seemed it wasn't my time just yet.

However I was not out of danger yet. The devastating news came that I had had a near-fatal stroke. This meant a lack of oxygen getting to my brain. They had to get me to hospital as quickly as possible, as I could be suffering brain damage or have a heart attack. All this seems so hazy now. I can remember being taken downstairs to the waiting ambulance and having an oxygen mask put on me as the paramedics began working on saving my life. I remember

4

them saying, 'We're going in on blues and twos'. It all seemed as if I was taking part in an episode of 'Casualty', or perhaps I had entered a parallel universe. How could I have had a stroke? I was fit and healthy, and I had never smoked. Would I survive?

I was rushed into the High Dependency Unit at the Royal Victoria Infirmary, still thinking I would wake up to find that this was all a horrible dream. But I was about to find out the true horror of what had happened to me.

It seemed my perfect service record had saved me, as the people at work had realised something serious must be wrong and put their life-saving procedure in place. I have my line manager and department manager to thank for saving my life.

Chapter 2

Hospital

The first task for the medical staff was to slow my heart rate down to reduce the risk of a heart attack. It was now I realised the serious of my position. Even if I made it, my life was going to be changed forever. I still couldn't feel or move my left side, and I felt I could have cried an ocean. I was told that my condition and what had happened to me would be fully explained by a doctor during his round. I hated hospitals, and now I was about to live in one, my worst nightmare.

When the doctor, a stroke specialist, came round, he explained everything to me, though I'm not sure I took it all in. How could this have happened? I had gone to bed feeling perfectly fine. I was fit and healthy and had always played by the rules. I had never smoked or taken drugs, and although I liked a drink, I ate healthily and kept fit. I had an active job, and remember I walked to and from work every day, a distance of around two and a half miles.

I was told that I had had a stroke on the right side of my brain, which controlled the left side of my body. I asked the doctor how long I would have to stay in hospital and what would happen to my life, but he just told me I would have to stay in hospital for the foreseeable future and would have rules and guidelines to follow.

While I had been in the ambulance I had had a catheter inserted to deal with my urine, and although it didn't give me any pain, just the thought of it brought tears to my eyes. In hospital I of course had to use the dreaded bedpan. For a bowel movement I had to be lifted using a Galvo hoist onto a commode, which made me feel like I was on a cheap fairground ride. I was labelled 'nil by mouth', which meant I couldn't eat or drink anything and had to receive all nourishment from a drip feed. I must have looked in a terrible state. I was surrounded by other patients who were mostly older than me, and so ill that I thought they would be lucky to survive another day. So what were my chances? I felt I was in a long, dark tunnel with little or no light at the end of it. It seemed I had entirely lost the use of the left side of my body. I thought the left side of my face had dropped slightly, and was told this was normal for a stroke victim. Thankfully my speech had remained unchanged, so I could communicate normally. This was because my stroke had been on the right side, while it is the left side that controls speech.

I have noticed that these days there is far more public awareness of strokes, with a TV campaign called FAST, which stands for Face/Arms/Speech/Time, the four critical factors in recognising and dealing with strokes. The quicker you act after seeing someone with signs of a stroke, the more of the person you save. That's fine if there is someone on hand who can recognise the signs and help you. The reason I was in such a bad way was that I had spent nearly 60 hours on the floor after falling when I had had the stroke and part of my brain had been starved of oxygen during that time. Another couple of hours and I would not be here to tell the story!

This is all part of the perils of living alone. Although I had a communal kitchen and living room, as soon as I shut the door to my flat I was alone.

Gail came to see me during those early days on the HDU and she must have been horrified at the sight of me. The fit man she had known as her husband was now in a hospital bed with tubes and wires sticking out of him. She seemed very caring, and I wondered why she couldn't have been like that when we were married. I suppose she must have been, at first. The cold fact was that I was an outside in her family home with her two sons.

My only other visitors were my bosses from work, Brian, my section manager, and Steve, the manager of my department. I had a good rapport with Steve through football. He supported Chesterfield while I supported my beloved Mansfield Town – the teams were fierce rivals – so this led to much banter.

When I had been on the HDU for just over a week, I was told that my heart rate had been brought down to a safe level and I was out of immediate danger. I was also told that I was going to be moved into a normal ward, Ward 43, an all-male ward. I still had all the rigmarole with the bedpan and the hoist, but I saw that this ward was visited by the food trolley. I couldn't remember the last time I had eaten normal food or what it was. Once the doctors and the stroke specialist thought it was safe for me to eat, I would have to pass a 'swallow test' to make sure I was not in danger of choking. If I passed it, the tubes and wires would be taken out and I would be allowed to eat and drink normally. For now though they remained in, so I still looked a horrific sight.

I can remember getting a surprise visit from my brother Darren and best pal Mark Frost, who had travelled up from Nottingham for the day to see me. That certainly gave me a lift. It was a nightmare being in a hospital so far from my home city of Nottingham. I regretted moving away from Nottingham and leaving behind all my friends there. I had spent 24 very happy years there and felt now that I should never have left. My nickname at work during those years had been 'the postman', because I always delivered!

I didn't have much family left in Nottingham, only my father and Darren. If I had had more family it would have been a much harder decision to move away. We lost our mother in 1971, when I was only six and Darren was only two. I have no memory of her.

Having a severe stroke must be one of the worst things that can happen to someone, as it takes away your life. I knew I had lost the life I had had, and I had no idea what the future held. Fortunately, although the stroke had affected my brain and my heart, my memory was still intact. It was explained to me that the stroke could have resulted in a neurological condition because of the areas of the brain I had lost. I would have a series of tests to find out what level of damage had been caused.

I was determined that this was not going to be the end of my life – there had to be a way back! After all I was still in my forties and I had been in good health until the stroke happened. I think the hospital knew from the outset that they had a very different stroke patient on their hands. I was never going to simply accept what had happened. They realised this when I kept asking for the swallow test, but they kept saying 'When we think you're ready'. I just replied every time that I WAS ready. The medical team, the doctors, nurses and consultants have the knowledge and the guidelines to follow, but they didn't know me! Even at this early stage I wanted to rip up their guidelines and become a survivor. I was determined to get my life back.

This strong will of mine and positive mental attitude must have played a big part in my recovery. Yes, I was still in a long dark tunnel with no light visible at the end, but the stroke had not changed me as a person. I was still strong-minded with a sense of humour, as when a nurse announced 'It's doctors' round' and I called back 'Good, I'll have a Jack Daniels and Coke!'

One thing that was different on the new ward was that each morning at 7 am the curtains would be drawn around my bed and two of the nurses would give me a 'bed bath', which was not really a bath but more of a wipe down with wet wipes and a bowl of water. I was also changed each morning into clean pants, jogging bottoms and a T-shirt. Gail was visiting regularly and bringing me new joggers and underwear. I couldn't help wondering why she couldn't have been like this during our eight years of marriage. I now had to wear pyjamas at night and was got ready for bed and 'lights out' by the evening nursing shift.

My brother Darren had told as many people as he could back in Nottingham about my devastating stroke, and he was going to put an update on his Facebook page now that he had been to see me. He came up with the idea that I should have regular contact with him so that he could keep everyone informed through Facebook. I did have my mobile phone in my cabinet along with a few other personal items the police had packed up in my room at the flat, and I agreed to send Darren a daily text update. His wife Donna was a nurse at the Queen's Medical Centre, the big main hospital in Nottingham, so she would understand any medical terms I used. However, when I tried to write a text message I had a problem. For some reason I had always used my left hand to text, but now I could no longer use my left hand or arm. I was going to have to try to learn to use my right hand. My first try was gobbledegook and nobody could have understood it.

After a few days of the staff on ward 43 listening to my moaning and groaning and demanding to be given the swallow test, they agreed to set up the test ahead of time. If I could pass it, it would be a victory for me. I would be able to smile and say 'I told you so!' And more importantly, I would be able to eat again. I didn't even consider failure, but if I did fail it would of course be the nurses and doctors saying 'I told you so'. I was determined not to give them that chance and let the wires stay attached to me.

The swallow test began with drinking a very small glass of water. I took my time with this and it went down fine. That was quite possibly the best drink I have ever had. Then it was onto the food. This started with the nurse feeding me a small spoonful of yoghurt. It was like being a baby again, at 48 years old. Like standing up and walking, I was going to have to learn all this again. It seemed so cruel that my life had been taken away like this.

Back to the swallow test. Next came a small piece of soft cake, and I managed that too. Finally came something harder, a dry biscuit. That went down as well. I had done it – I had passed the test. I had scored a vital victory. That was my first battle won. I would face many, many more on my long road to recovery, but at least I was now on that road. Now I would be able to have the wires and the drip removed and there would be no more of the crap they were pumping into me. I would be able to eat and drink normally.

There were three meals a day at the RVI, breakfast, lunch and dinner. Hospitals are not known for the quality of their food, which has been the butt of many jokes, but let me tell you, when you haven't eaten normal food for many weeks, any food tastes wonderful.

Now that I was able to eat at last, I was ready for anything and everything they gave me. I soon began to feel that I was regaining my strength. I didn't know how long I had been in the RVI, but it was beginning to feel like a lifetime, yet it all still seemed unreal. My old world seemed like another lifetime. My life had changed forever and was now going to be very different. I didn't know what future lay ahead for me – or even if I had a future.

As I gained strength, I was told that I was ready to start my rehabilitation programme. This would include physio sessions and working with a team of occupational therapists, all specialists. This would not take place at the RVI but at a unit called the Cherryburn Stroke Unit on the site of the former general hospital on Westgate Road, which was now closed. The unit was near to my old marital home, and even nearer to the shared house I had been living in.

As always in the NHS you have to wait, so I now had to wait for a bed to become available at the Cherryburn. With my transfer pending, I was told to pack up my clothing and the few personal items which the nurses had packed up for me on the ward. Because of my condition I had to be transferred on a trolley by ambulance. So it was goodbye to the RVI at last. I didn't see this as a step forward, just a shuffle sideways.

Chapter 3

Dark days

It was the early hours of an October morning when my transfer to the Cherryburn Stroke Unit came through. Although I was in a bit of a daze, I can remember being greeted at the main door by a male staff nurse, Paul – at least they were expecting me. I remember the ambulance crew wheeling me into a large room to Bed 10, lifting me onto the bed and shutting the door behind them on their way out. All was quiet, and I was on my own. I felt isolated, and I could have cried an ocean.

I don't recall sleeping much in my new surroundings, just waiting for the day to start. When daylight came at last, my room seemed fine and large. I had two big wardrobes with a view onto a garden and a prickly hedge. In the room I had my own wardrobe, a small chest of drawers and nothing else except the plain cream-painted walls, and of course the bed I was in. It felt like a prison cell. Was this the end? Was that why they had put me in here?

During that first day I started to meet the new team of nurses, starting with the two doing the early morning round. I remember they had the same name, but I don't recall what it was. Here I would have my own dedicated stroke doctor, Dr Luwe, pronounced 'Lowe', who was originally from South Africa. I got to meet the physio team and was pushed along the corridors in a wheelchair by my own personal physiotherapist, Jenny. All the walls were painted the same bland cream, and it seemed a desolate place. Nothing had yet changed in my circumstances, and I still had a catheter. I was still only allowed to be hoisted from my bed on a Galvo hoist and I was still having to use the commode.

They did have a dining room here, where the three daily meals were served, and this was where the patients got to meet each other, everyone being pushed to the dining room in wheelchairs by members of staff. Wherever you went, you had to be pushed there in a wheelchair by a nurse. We were all in the same boat here. The unit wasn't a large place – there were four main corridors arranged almost in a square, on one of which was my room. There was a TV room with seating for patients, relatives and visitors (most of the patients were a lot older than me). This and the dining room had views out onto a garden, which was on the other side of the building to my room. The garden and the outside world seemed far away, like a distant galaxy. All this was alien to me, as before my stroke I had spent hardly any time in hospital and had always been so healthy. I had only previously been in hospitals when I was visiting someone, and even then I had not liked them.

But this was to be my home for the next four months. Dark days lay ahead as I entered a new chapter in my long road back to recovery. But at least here I would get the physiotherapy and all the other help I needed to help me to learn to walk again. Jenny told me however that they could not guarantee this – in fact nothing could be guaranteed. If I didn't manage to walk again I would have to spend the rest of my life in a wheelchair and possibly being looked after in a care home. For me that would mean my life was over. I felt it was so unfair. I felt like hating the world and saying, 'why me?' but I knew that the more I did this the more it would drive me crazy.

Anyway, before I could think of learning to walk again I had to learn to stand up. This would be done in my physio sessions. I was also going to work with the occupational therapy team, headed by Ivy. Thanks to my Nottingham accent this came out as 'Iveh', which seemed to amuse the staff. I was going to have physio and occupational therapy (OT) sessions once a day, and I would be fetched for each session by a member of the team, then wheeled back again. This would help to fill up my days, which was good news as the days in the hospital felt so long. However there would be no sessions on a Saturday or Sunday, as this part of the Cherryburn didn't work at weekends.

It all seemed very organised. The times of my physio and OT sessions were put up on a large notice board in the main corridor which told all patients where they were supposed to be at what time. The main corridor also contained the nurses' station and a small room where they took their breaks. There was also a small concrete patio area with bench seating, much like the benches you find in a pub garden. This area was not far from my room in the main corridor', the 'corridor of power', as I called it. My room, actually Bed 10, was one of a total of 22. I was lucky to have a room to myself as most of the rooms had more than one bed in them. This was because my room had an oxygen supply, in case I needed it. There was a physio room, known as the gym, and rooms for the OT sessions, plus a couple of meeting rooms where patients could meet staff or have visitors. These had large comfortable chairs, plus a couple of tables with chairs round them, which provided more comfortable surroundings than the Ward Sister's office.

As I got to know the staff I began to learn about the different uniforms. A blue uniform indicated that the wearer was fully trained and allowed to administer medication.

Those wearing brown were still in training. The three male nurses wore white coats, which made them look ice cream sellers. Two of them were called Keith, so they soon became known as Big Keith and Little Keith. These two mainly worked on the night shift. The third, Paul, was the one who had met me at the entrance upon my arrival. I liked Paul and the stories he would tell every day about his cat Colin. Of the nurses my favourite was Kayleigh, who wore a blue uniform and was tall, slim, blonde and very attractive.

Mealtimes were set in stone – the same time each day. You couldn't miss out, as a member of staff would come to fetch you, hoist you out of bed, get you into a wheelchair and push you to the dining room.

Breakfast was between 7 and 7.30 and consisted of cereal followed by toast with a choice of jam or marmalade, all spread on for you, washed down by coffee or tea served by the nurses, another part of their daily routine. If Kayleigh was serving breakfast I could have as much toast as I wanted. She seemed to enjoy looking after me. I think she liked having someone younger as a patient, as most of the others were older and had seemed to give up on life following strokes late in their lives. I was going to fight back – I wanted my life back!

Lunch, the main meal of the day, was at 12 noon, and dinner was usually some kind of pie with potatoes and vegetables. Again I was very well looked after by Kayleigh and given extra gravy. My favourite meal was on a Sunday, when we got roast lamb. If Kayleigh was serving I would sometimes get second helpings, and even sometimes had two dinners! This was recorded, as most things are in a hospital, all noted on a clipboard that hung at the end of your bed (Kayleigh showed it to me one day). So was your sleeping pattern. I did not realise at first that the nurses would come round during the night and check by torchlight what position you were sleeping in, ie on your back, or which side you were lying on.

The last meal of the day was afternoon tea, served at 5 pm. This was soup followed by sandwiches (my favourite was cheese and pickle) and then cake with cream, all washed down with coffee or tea.

After each meal the medication trolley came round. Only the nurses in blue uniforms were able to give medication. The nurses worked so hard, doing such long hours – I didn't realise they did so much. They had so many different tasks, such as serving meals three times a day. It wasn't just about their actual nursing duties.

I always had my meals at the same time and took my medication at the same time – if it works, why change it? I still do to this day. My last tablet of the day was taken when the medication trolley came round to the room between 9 and 10 pm, usually brought by Big Keith or Little Keith. This was also lights out time, and afterwards everything went dark and silent.

The location of the Cherryburn Stroke Unit meant that

my new love Lexi could call in and see me as she passed by on her way home from work. Like me she worked at John Lewis; we had met during the last years of my ever-deteriorating marriage. It wasn't like an affair – she did still have a partner. I saw it more like when you change trains at a station to find your next train is already on the platform, waiting for you. I felt sorry for Lexi as she had been on holiday on the Greek island of Crete when I had my stroke and she had no idea what had happened and had to walk back in to see this awful mess on her return home.

Now that Lexi was visiting me I could have some books brought to me from my room at home, which was only a few streets away. I was still paying rent to the letting agency and all my belongings were still there. I had no trouble paying the rent as I was on full sick pay, and as I was in hospital I wasn't spending anything. I gave Lexi my key so she could not only bring books for me but do my laundry and swap some of my clothes around, bless her.

During our short time together we had made plans to run away to a Greek island and have our happy ever after there. We had even signed up for a Greek language class together, but the stroke had put an end to all that. For now Lexi was standing by me and coming to see me. She was still going to the Greek class and bringing me Greek 'homework' to do in hospital, then taking it back to Anastasia, our teacher.

I had to make sure Lexi's visits did not clash with those of Gail, who was still my wife, although I had moved out of the marital home the previous July. That now seemed a lifetime ago. I was going to get a divorce and run away with Lexi, our own fairytale, once she had left her partner. I still wanted to see her and she was still standing by me but the visiting times made it difficult as she was often at work. She would come to see me on a Wednesday afternoon on her way home, bringing me work from the previous evening's Greek class. We didn't get much time together as visiting time finished before afternoon tea was served at 5 pm. I went to see Claire, the ward sister and manager of the unit, to explain the situation and ask if they would allow Lexi to visit me on a Saturday evening. Thankfully she understood, as she had seen us together and could see that we loved each other. She was happy to make a special arrangement for Lexi to visit at 8 pm for an hour on Saturday evenings. This became known as 'date night' among the staff, and Claire held a meeting with them to explain my special situation.

It was wonderful to have that hour with Lexi, but so difficult to watch her leave. She would take away my completed coursework to hand to Anastasia, my efforts would be marked and brought back the following Wednesday with the next week's work.

I found it difficult to concentrate on the coursework in the quiet of my room and found that my eyes began to hurt and I would get tired and start getting a headache within 15 minutes or so. This was a result of the damage to my brain caused by the stroke. Before I had my stroke the word 'neurology' was just a term I had seen on hospital signs, but I found it fascinating to discover what the human brain can do. The hope was that with the help of the occupational therapist my brain would rewire itself; as areas affected by the stroke were lost, other parts of my brain would take over the work of the affected areas and learn to do what they could no longer do. I had to try to learn to stand up and walk again, but there was no guarantee that I would be able to. This was what I would be doing with the Cherryburn physio team, during my daily physio sessions. I could have lost the ability to think clearly or work things out, such as problem solving or puzzles. This I would be tackling with the OT (occupational therapy) team. I was shown a model of the human brain, intact and then how it looked after a stroke – the affected area was black and dead.

The therapy teams worked 9 to 5 on weekdays and had the weekends off, whereas the nurses had to cover a full-time rota, 24 hours a day, seven days a week.

My first few sessions of physio in the gym room were devoted to getting me to stand up for the first time since my stroke. I can remember Jenny telling me 'find your middle', meaning stand up straight, as I tried to stand up straight with the help of two physiotherapists, one each side so I didn't fall. They stood me in front of a tall dressing mirror so that I could see how straight I was, but I could not stop wobbling and leaning. I felt like a toddler trying to stand up for the first time and wobbling while he tries to find his balance. I was having to learn to stand again as if I was a baby. It took some time before I was able to stand up on my own again, but I had plenty of time – I wasn't going anywhere in a hurry.

Next came learning how to side-step, starting with just a few paces at first, again with a physiotherapist either side of me, until I could get across part of the floor and then safely cross from one side of the gym room to the other. It was very early days still, but at least I was now on that long road to recovery. My long journey towards rehabilitation had begun - I had begun to fight back. Jenny and her team could see my determination and positive mindset and knew I wanted my life back.

Over my four long months at the Cherryburn Stroke Unit I would learn to walk again, starting with a few steps in the gym room before being allowed to walk along the unit's four corridors. First I would walk halfway down the first corridor, with a nurse in front of me, another behind and one either side – it was like flying with the Red Arrows! Jenny would walk with me, barking out instructions for when to move my left leg. The corridors were always kept clear of obstructions to ensure there was nothing to fall over. In time the aim was for me to walk the full length of the corridor, then two, then three and finally all four, always with the team in flying formation around me, until I could walk without supervision. My progress would attract a lot of attention. In time I would be able to leave the gym room and walk back to my room.

Although I found reading difficult and it made me tired and gave me headaches, I persisted with it as it is something I have always enjoyed, and gradually I was able to read for longer without my eyes hurting. It certainly helped to pass the long days in hospital. I was still doing my homework for the Greek class, and my concentration levels were improving, so I was making slow but steady progress.

I was also making progress in my physio and OT sessions, and was assigned a social worker, Alison, and a clinical psychologist called Helen who I would see on a daily basis in between my physio and OT sessions. This was to watch for any signs of depression or anger develop in the aftermath of what had happened. It would have been so easy to be angry at the world, and I did feel that way at times, but I wanted to channel the anger in a positive way. The only way to do that was to look forward, adopt a positive mental attitude and fight back. Looking back and wondering why it had happened would surely have driven me crazy. I think that's why, when a devastating life event happens, you are assigned these specialists. But I felt I didn't need them – I was going to walk out of there all on my own! I felt desperate at times to get out of that desolate place.

Although I felt I did not need these meetings with Alison and Helen, I had to go along with them. By some quirk of fate one day, while I was talking to Alison, the bookmark fell out of the book I was reading, which was Michael Palin's *Around the World in 80 Days*. On the bookmark was a photo of two sun loungers against the backdrop of the beautiful blue Mediterranean.

'That looks fabulous,' said Alison, picking up the photo.

'Thats where I want to be,' I replied.

'Oh David, those days are long gone,' she said. So much for a positive and helpful social worker. I made up my mind that I was going to see that lovely blue sea again somehow, some day. I had found a new inspiration and a new motivation for my recovery, and that's why I wanted a picture like that to be on the cover of this book. I was determined to prove her and everybody else wrong, and I was going to continue learning Greek despite my condition.

My work with Ivy, the occupational therapist assigned to me, was going very well and I was making good progress there too. We were working on the neurological condition the stroke had left me with to see just how much I had lost, as nobody yet knew – every stroke victim is different. This meant doing word searches, sudoku, solving join-up-the-dots puzzles, and drawing clocks (lots of clocks!) and then filling in the time. The Occupational Therapy Service seemed to like clocks! I had no problem with any of these. I also had to work at solving problems using what look like children's building blocks, having to fit different-shaped pegs into the rights holes and so on. I was given time to work these out, then marked accordingly. Ivy explained that many stroke victims lose the ability to solve problems and perform these tasks, and suffer memory loss. I had not, thankfully – I was going to be a stroke survivor. I dread to think what life would be like if you lost your memory and could not manage these tasks.

Then, just when I thought life could not get any worse, it did. On the morning of October 11, the news came from my younger brother Darren in Nottingham that our father had died. Now I began to question life. What had I done to deserve this, and why was the world suddenly so against me? Why do some people seem to glide through life with ease, while mine seemed to be full of potholes? I was still trying to come to terms with what had happened to me when I got this news. Dad was old at 82 and frail, and he had been ill for some time, but it was still a terrible shock.

I told the unit about this news and said I wanted to go to my dad's funeral. In my absence, Darren would have to arrange everything. I felt for him, as it should have been me as the older brother.

All this was a huge blow to my rehabilitation, but more bad news was to come. Claire summoned me into her office to ask me how I was feeling about this news. I told her I wanted to go to the funeral, but she told me this would not be possible as I was still in a wheelchair and still had to be hoisted around as I couldn't stand. I was told to forget the idea, as I had no hope of going. Claire was upset at having to tell me this. I felt that I had lost my life as I had known it and now I had lost my dad as well, all in the space of two months. Surely it is every man's right to go to his parents' funeral, but that right had been cruelly taken away. Again I found myself questioning the world and asking why it was so against me all of a sudden. I was glad I did not believe in God, because why would he let these things happen to me? I could feel my world collapsing around me. Back in September when Lexi had gone on her holiday, I had felt I had the world at my feet and was looking forward to love starting up again on her return. It was very difficult saying goodbye to Lexi for her two-week holiday to Crete. When she had gone away we had had our lives ahead of us, but now it was all in bits.

The news of my dad's death seemed to be a huge game-changer as things started to happen in my daily physio sessions. I was learning to stand on my own again by the end of October. Not only was I able to stand, I also learned to side-step. I could only do a few paces in both directions, but it was progress. Next I would learn to walk again, with the help of the physio team. I was now fighting back. I seemed to be using the news of my dad's death as some kind of inspiration, but my clinical psychologist and social worker were concerned for me with the events happening in my life. Perhaps they were looking for signs of depression. Depression, me? I told them both that depression is a very bad thing. It's like a virus that spreads through the mind, then one morning you wake up and become a Notts County fan...

Perhaps they both wanted me to give up, like a lot of patients on the unit. It seemed easier for everyone for me to give up, then they could sit me in a wheelchair and put me in front of the television to rot rather than fight back as I was doing.

I again showed Sharon my photograph of the Mediterranean and the sun loungers and her reply was, 'I've told you to forget about things like that'. I had no hope of going. I was starting to get fed up of hearing those words. I don't know why there were so negative when I wanted to be so positive – perhaps they wanted to keep patients' feet on the ground.

After the week I had had I was so looking forward to seeing Lexi on the Saturday evening for our 'date night – I needed a hug – we all do at times.

The news came from my brother that our dad's funeral was going to be on November 8 with a service at the church near his home in Carlton before he as buried in Carlton Cemetery, followed by a wake at his club, the Richard Herod Bowls Centre. My brother had made the arrangements. The coffin would stop outside 49 Valley Road, Carlton, where my brother and I grew up and spent many happy years. But even though I was making good progress, I was still told I wouldn't be able to go. Again I was summoned into Claire's office, where she explained the decision. How would I get to Nottingham, and where would I stay? Who would look after me? Even though I was doing well in my physio sessions I still needed round-the-clock care and help with toileting. To be honest, once it was explained to me why I wasn't being allowed to go to my own dad's funeral I did understand, but it didn't stop the hurt and pain I felt, and I still questioned the world.

Each morning a couple of nurses would come around the stroke unit and come into patients' rooms, taking and recording each patient's sats, which means oxygen levels, heart rate, temperature and blood pressure. Mine was usually low, meaning I wasn't drinking enough water. Like all the patients I had a jug of water on the table in my room, kept full by the nurses. I must admit I had never heard of low blood pressure, only high, but I was told low BP is equally dangerous. I had to make sure I drank more water, and when Lexi heard this she started bringing me bottles of squash and getting the nurses to add it to the water jug. Sure enough in time my blood pressure did creep up until it reached an almost perfect reading. That was what I needed if I was ever going to get out of there.

Probably because I was still using my dad's death as motivation I continued to make good progress during

November and could feel I was getting stronger. Physio was going well with much improvement, as were my occupational therapy sessions. I was also getting more visitors, which cheered me up as I was now able to hold longer conversations without getting a headache and feeling tired. I could also show my visitors and friends that I was able to stand upright and stay steady. I was also able to get off my bed and stand upright, but I needed help to get back onto or into bed. My stroke doctor, Dr Luwe, who came to see me on his rounds each Friday, was very impressed by my progress. As always Lexi would visit often, and now my friends from work, David, Billy and Ricey, were visiting me regularly. It was great to see them as they brought chocolate and biscuits!

I asked for time to myself on the day of the funeral, November 8, with no visitors. Having wanted to be along I asked for my dinner to be brought to my room, as I didn't feel like going into the dining room with all the other patients. As it was a Friday this meant the meal was fish and chips, the only meal I didn't enjoy as it was like cardboard, dry and tasteless. Otherwise I was eating well. I had always been a big eater and I had not lost any of my appetite, but even I couldn't eat cardboard fish! Even trying to smother it in tomato sauce didn't help. If you needed anything you could press the call button, which was attached by a cord so you could keep it beside you in the bed. In an emergency you could pull the cord and someone would come to see what you wanted. I had to pull it once when my legs gave way and I fell onto the floor, and within seconds help had arrived. That was a reminder that however well I thought I was doing, I was still in a bad way. It made me realise that they were right in not letting me go to the funeral.

Also on the wall was a double plug socket, so I could charge my mobile phone. I had taught myself to text with my right hand. I now even had permission to phone Lexi on her breaks at work – she had breaks at the same time each day. It was good to be able to hear her voice, sometimes twice a day.

My dad must have known he was going to die, as he wrote a letter and put it an envelope addressed to Darren with the words 'only open after my death'. Darren had kept his promise not to open it, though I'm not sure I would have done the same. In the letter he made known what he wanted to be done at his funeral, a church service followed by burial (not that he ever went to church). He also stated that he wanted everyone to wear something red, the colour of Nottingham Forest! He had been a Forest nut all his life. Football had always been a big part of the Morris household. It was what linked us together. Like any footballing father, I think his biggest delight was taking Darren and me down to the City ground. I saw two very successful European Cup years (now called the Champions' League) when Forest won, in 1979 and 1980.

Later I became a season ticket holder. I lasted longer than Darren, who sadly became a Notts County fan!

In 1981, after I had started work and had money for myself and my own opinion, I saw sense and became a Mansfield Town fan, and I still am to this day, but I still have Forest blood in me as it's the first result I look for in the newspaper.

If I had been able to go to my dad's funeral I wouldn't have worn red but the yellow football shirt of my beloved Mansfield Town. This was not to go against his wishes and disrespect him – he may well have expected it from me and found it amusing. He would have smiled and said in his deep voice, 'There's always one prat'.

I still have fond memories of my trips to Wembley Stadium with him. Sometimes I would make my own way to London, meeting him in his favourite pub there, the Green Man. One time Nottingham Forest played Luton Town in a cup final in Luton, the home of the 'Hatters'. Dad still went to Wembley that day with his Forest bowler hat and cane, and they were put in the coffin with him. In the Green Man that day he was getting some banter from the Luton fans. Dad had great delight in telling the large crowd of Luton fans that his hat and cane had gone to Wembley in 1959 when Forest had won the FA Cup against Luton Town! He was outnumbered many times over, but it didn't bother him as he was a big character.

I think the worst part of losing someone is the feeling that you will never get to see them again or hear their voice. My dad had died not knowing what had happened to me because he was very ill. We kept it from him, as it could have finished him off. Perhaps it did – maybe he knew. I had been close myself, but I guess September 2013 wasn't my time.

In June that year my Dad had asked me to come down to Nottingham for the weekend for Father's Day and get together with him and Darren. I now wonder if he knew it was the last chance we would have to be together. Did he know his time was near? Donna, Darren's wife, took a photo of the three of us together and that was the last picture ever taken of us together, so I regard it as priceless. I didn't take Gail that weekend because of her drinking problem, as I didn't want any trouble on Dad's special day. Gail couldn't control her drink – it controlled her. She would regularly drink a bottle of vodka when she got home from work, then turn nasty and volatile. This also happened if we went out on a weekend away or even holidays, so I stopped taking her, and if I went away it would be on my own. I think the biggest problem with someone with a drink problem is getting them to admit it and see just what it doing to them and those around them. I lost count of the number of times she phoned the police on me saying I had threatened her. I was taller, bigger and stronger than her and I had to push her away when she came for me as if she was a dog with rabies. The police would come and see that she had been drinking, but it was me who had to leave the house. I would stay in a hotel for a few nights and go back when she had calmed down. I couldn't live like that for much longer. We got married in June 2005 and I should have walked away in August 2008. Yet I had never seen this side of her before I married her, or I would never have done it.

As the calendar turned over into December I realised I would be there for Christmas and into my third month away from society. Christmas is supposed to be the most wonderful time of the year, but not for me that that year. However I managed to use this to summon up some new-found determination. I told myself I might be there for Christmas, but I wasn't going to be there for my birthday in February!

The month of December turned out to be a huge one for me and I now wanted to get out of the Cherryburn Stroke Unit. I was now improving each day and so much seemed to happen. First I had the catheter removed, so I could pee naturally into a cardboard bottle as I lay in bed. I came off the Galvo hoist and was now using a standing hoist called an Arjo. I nickname the Arjo Ned, as it felt like I was standing on the back of a horse. It made Kayleigh smile and she started calling it Ned too. Using Ned I stood on the footplates at the back leaning over and a nurse would help me put my hands on the handles at the front of the Arjo. The front did look like a horse's head with the handles being the ears, and when I leaned over I looked like a jockey. It only needed one nurse to operate the Arjo, so it was also better for the nurses as they pulled it behind them, like a stable girl leading a horse by its reins.

I texted this news to Darren, knowing that Donna would be able to explain it to him as she had been a nurse at the Queen's Medical Centre in Nottingham and had operated one herself.

Using the Arjo was a huge step forward and made a big improvement to life in the unit as it meant I didn't have to use the commode any more. Ned would take me to the toilet and the nurse would lift me down onto the toilet seat. When I had finished I would pull a red cord and a nurse would come in and clean me, without me losing all my dignity.

Because I was making progress I was now moved from bed 10 to bed 2 along the same corridor. This bed was in a large room shared with bed 1 – yes, I was going to have to share with another horrible stroke patient. In total I had four 'roommates', three of whom I couldn't get on with at all. They were all such negative people who seemed to have given up on life and didn't want to recover. It seemed they wanted to stay in the until the end, whenever that came. I on the other hand wanted out! I complained to Claire that I didn't want people like this around me and felt it could hinder my progress. She understood this. When I asked why I had had to be moved, I was told bed 10 had a supply of oxygen which I no longer needed, so it was required for a new patient who would need it.

The only 'roomie' I got on well with was Harry Knox, who was much older than me, more my dad's age at 80. Harry had a good mindset and he too wanted to get out and enjoy the rest of his life, however long that might be.

No matter how hard all the staff tried, hospital is not the place to be at Christmas, though the unit did look nice, with large Christmas trees at the entrance and in reception and another in the patients' dining room. I wanted to cry an ocean at being there over the festive period, but I must say that all the nursing staff were fantastic. They made sure that every patient had a present to open on Christmas Day. The male patients got a set of Lynx shower gel and body spray and the women got a Dove or Nivea set. These came out of the nurses' own pockets – they had a collection between them. That's not the sort of story you usually hear about with the NHS, as normally the press has only negative news.

All the patients sat down together for Christmas dinner, pulling crackers and wearing the party hats from out of them. We were allowed some wine with our meal, a glass with our Christmas dinner (this came down from the management). When Kayleigh poured my wine I wanted a Christmas kiss, but this would not have been acceptable. At least I thought about it, and it's the thought that counts.

For some reason the Salvation Army and Christmas

seem to go together, and everyone seems to think of them at this time of year. During our Christmas afternoon tea of sandwiches and mince pies, they came in and played carols. While they were playing I seemed to forget about the horrible situation I was in for a moment. A sprinkling of Christmas cheer can go a long way, specially when it's accompanied by a smile from the gorgeous Kayleigh, and I will long remember that Christmas of 2013.

I had a nice surprise on Christmas afternoon. I wasn't expecting any visitors, but my friends David and Stephen came to visit me. We got on well as we all had the same dry sense of humour and I so enjoyed their tales about when they had worked for BA as cabin crew. Lexi had told me with regret that she wouldn't be able to visit me over Christmas due to family commitments, but she did! She came on Christmas Eve, bringing a couple of presents. I felt bad that I had not got her anything, but how could I? She understood. It was again a lovely surprise to see her, my new love.

It's said that miracles happen at Christmas, and I was starting to have my own. I was starting to learn to walk again, and by Christmas Eve I could walk from the gym room to my new room. It's a shame I didn't have any physio over the next two days, as on Christmas Day and Boxing Day the physio team didn't work, as at weekends.

I recall an interesting moment on Boxing Day. While having some time to myself in one of the meeting rooms I was also catching up with some of my Greek homework. It had become more difficult now that I had to share a room. One of the older nurses came into the room (her name was Wright, and she would say that was because she was always right, which made me laugh). She wanted to know what I was doing, so I explained and showed her my work. I was amazed by her response. She said she used to live on the Greek island of Kefalonia, and had owned a bar there for many years. Some of the film *Captain Corelli's Mandolin* was filmed in her bar, and she even met the star, Nicolas Cage. The film had made the island famous and many people wanted to visit it, just as had happened years earlier with the film *Shirley Valentine* and Mykonos, and more recently with *Mamma Mia* and Skopalos.

I found listening to Mrs Wright so interesting. She could help me with my Greek.

I spent New Year's Eve in bed listening to BBC Radio Five Live on my pocket radio through my earphones, with reporters seeing in the New Year from countries around the world as the New Year started in each of them. I was glad to see the back of 2013!

The New Year of 2014 was going to bring new hope. My walking was getting better, and I could walk down one corridor with the physio team around me, but no longer assisting me. Soon I could manage two corridors, then finally all four, as long as I had somebody behind me. This was huge news, but the bad news was that I still had no movement in my left arm, which just sat across my chest. I was told that this might never come back, and I might never have natural movement in that arm again, because of the amount of time I had been lying on the floor following the stroke. That was a devastating blow. So I still had dark days ahead. What sort of quality of life could I expect without the use of my left arm? Once again, I wanted to sit in a corner of the room and cry an ocean.

Something else I couldn't do was to sit on a large gym ball with my legs either side without wobbling all over the place or worse, falling off. The idea of this was to help with my balance. Now the physio sessions had started again – after the holiday was over I would be working on and with the gym ball with Jenny, my physiotherapist. My occupational therapy session also restarted, with the devastating confirmation of the news that I would never be able to move my left arm again. I would have to learn to dress myself in a new way, with just my right arm. Dressing practice would take place in my room with Andy, the only male on the two trams of physios and occupational therapists. I told Andy he was a lucky man to be working alongside such lovely girls, but he didn't seem to agree.

For the moment I would still be dressed by the team of nurses during the morning rounds, or after the wake-up call at 6.45 which was also when I had a bed bath, or more accurately a bed wipe. They would dress you so you were ready to be taken down for breakfast at 7 am. My dressing practice sessions would also include learning how to wash myself again, using only my right arm, for which I was taken into the shower by two or three nurses, for safety reasons in case I fell. Although I could now stand up I still had to work on my balance, and I was going to be using the gym ball in the physio session. I realised that everything was done to fit in alongside each session as all the specialists bring everything together. In time I would be able to shower myself and dress myself alone. It would take time, but I had plenty of that.

The early days of January did bring much progress and improvement, and with it a new hope. Like a phoenix rising from the ashes, I was recovering fast. I was steadier on my feet and much stronger in balancing. I now no longer needed any kind of hoist. I could take myself down to the dining room, and most importantly I could take myself to the loo! I was still in that long, dark tunnel, but now I could see a faint light at the end of it.

My progress included mastering that gym ball, and I had been learning how to wash myself in the shower again. They gave me a stool in case I needed it. I had enjoyed being showered by three nurses, so getting better did have its drawbacks!

Jenny, my physiotherapist, told me I was ready for the next phase in physio sessions, which was how to get in and out of a car. I had to learn a very different way of doing this from the one I had been used to. I had to get in bum first, then swing my legs around, right leg first, often having to help the left leg. If I could pass this test I could be taken out for a short drive by a friend, but I would have to be in a wheelchair. The stroke unit had given me my own folding wheelchair for this purpose. Surely now it would be only a matter of time before I would be able to escape from the Cherryburn Stroke Unit. I had come so far in a very short space of time, but I still had a long way to go.

During one of my Friday meetings with Dr Luwe he told me 'You will beat this'. On another visit he had a colleague with him, and what this man said took me by surprise. After examining me he said my heart was still beating irregularly, and then told me this could be put right by stopping it and starting it again!

'You're not f***** doing that!' I told Dr Luwe. He explained that I could live with an irregular heartbeat if necessary, so that's what I decided to do. I did agree to a visit back to the RVI for some time in the cardiology department. I think my reaction shocked Dr Luwe. Having my heart stopped sounded too scary and risky. He and his team might be the specialists in this, but I was the patient – it was my body and my life! Dr Luwe did come back to see me and I apologised for swearing at him. He was fine about it and agreed that in the circumstances it should have been discussed.

He sat down with me to tell me what was involved. They would stop my heart and restart it using the electronic pads, placed on each side of the chest to give the body a powerful electric shock. My answer was still no! He said he would inform his colleague Dr Irvine at the RVI and make an appointment for me to see him to make sure everything was fine. I could have an echo scan, be wired up to an ECG machine to make sure that everything was fine with my heart. If I got the all clear it was another step closer to getting out of there. I would be taken to the RVI with a nurse from the stroke unit in a wheelchair taxi. My visit to the RVI was arranged for the following week.

The wheelchair taxi looked like the Popemobile! I was pushed up the ramp by the driver and into the back of the taxi so that I was sitting high above the driver, with Robyn, the young nurse who was taking me. I even did some waving on the journey, like the Pope! Robyn knew her way around and we found the cardiology department fairly quickly. We soon found ourselves in a medical room with Dr Irvine and a nurse. I had an Echo scan and hear my heart beating for the first time. It was not the 'boom boom' sound I expected but a sloshy, sloppy sound. Dr Irvine was busy looking at monitors and I caught sight of a shadowy shape – this was my heart. The results came back positive. The stroke had not damaged my heart and the chambers and valves were clear.

Dr Irvine gave Robyn a folder containing the results of the tests. It all seemed to be over quite quickly, but when I looked at the clock I saw that I had been there for 45 minutes. I could have done with popping to the RVI café for a coffee, but Robyn did things by the book and she said this was not allowed. She had to get me back to the stroke unit.

I now began to believe that I could beat this and have a life again eventually, although it would of course be very different from my previous life. I was determined to make the most of it. Things were coming together very well, and we began to talk about a release date. I was going to get out of there!

My good friend David was now helping with the car transfers. After passing Jenny's test and getting permission from her and Claire, I could now go out for short periods in his car, although this had to be in a wheelchair. The stroke unit had given me my own folding wheelchair, which David would fold down and put in the boot of his car. He drove me out to a pub called the Badger at Ponteland near Newcastle Airport, and it felt great to be able to go out like this, my first shot at being in society again. I have so much to thank David for. I could never have got to where I am today without him, like several of the people in this book – I owe them all so much.

The whole process started again when David took me back to the stroke unit. The trip had gone well and proved that I could go out and be brought back safely and was strong enough to go out for a short time. As David earned Jenny's trust he was allowed to take me out regularly after that, each time going to the Badger. I did however feel for my good friend, having to set up and fold down the wheelchair each time – it didn't seem fair that he had to do this, even though he was happy to. I am sure it had hurt David to see me like that. It was such a contrast with the person he knew at work, where I had always been active, carrying boxes about and always dashing off somewhere.

Now that my trips out were going well, I wanted to know if I could start going back to my Greek class on a Tuesday evening and get to spend time with Lexi. But once again this caused a problem, and I had another barrier in front of me. The Greek class was held in the Simply Greek restaurant in the big market area in the centre of Newcastle. There were steps down to it and I could not walk up or down steps, so I was told I couldn't go. So unfair! I asked if I could try and learn to negotiate steps, as I had achieved every other challenge that had been put in front of me, but the stroke unit was reluctant. There were no stairs in the unit, which of course was what stroke patients needed.

I found myself challenging the unit and its management again. I wanted to do stairs! I wanted to go to my Greek class! I wanted time with Lexi!

After some discussions with the so-called specialists, even Sharon, my social worker, and Helen, the clinical psychologist, got involved. I was told to report to the meeting room, large room between the gym room and the large room where my OT sessions were held. Waiting there for me were Jenny, her boss, the manager of the physio and OT teams, Hilary, plus Dr Luwe. It felt as if I was being put on trial, and this was the jury. I had not met Hilary before – in fact I had never heard of her. I was told to sit down and it felt as if I was going to be sentenced! Instead I was given what felt like a dressing down, with Hilary firing bullets at me. I had my say, telling them why I wanted to do stairs. I was told that in general, stroke victims do not go anywhere near stairs again. I told them, not for the first time, that I was a survivor, not a victim. Dr Luwe seemed to be on my side, and he asked how I proposed to get myself to the restaurant and at what times.

'By taxi,' I told him. 'The class is on for two hours, between 6 and 8 in the evening.'

This seemed to cause outrage. Hilary said I would have to be collected at the entrance. I told them Lexi would meet me outside the restaurant when I got out of the taxi and bring me back to the Cherryburn afterwards. She couldn't collect me to take me to the class as there wasn't time after she finished work at 5. I explained that at no time would I be on my own, if that was what they were worried about. I understood they had guidelines to follow and a 'rule book', although not for the first time, I wanted to rip it up!

We seemed to finish the meeting with a draw, but a replay was needed. They wanted to see Lexi at the next meeting, which meant she would have to take time away from work. At this meeting Claire, Ivy and Sharon would also be present.

I spoke with Lexi on the phone and we arranged to meet at the main entrance. We would then walk hand in hand along the corridor and into the room, where everybody would be waiting for us. I thought this would make a good impression, a sign that we loved each other and wanted to spend time together. It was going to be me and Lexi against the world! No wonder our special song was 'Against All Odds' by Phil Collins.

For the next week my physio session were going to be held in another part of the stroke unit, which I hadn't seen; it was part of the old general hospital building on the site of which the unit stood. This part of the building had a staircase which led to a basement which had been the maternity ward of the old hospital and was dark and spooky. The corridor was dark green, in contrast to the cream of the corridors of the stroke unit, and it was as if this place had been abandoned, an area that time forgot. On the dark green walls were pictures drawn in colouring pencils.

My task was to go down the stairs and back up, with Jenny at my side. At first I couldn't manage them, and was holding on to the handrail on the right side of the stairwell. But sheer determination had got me this far, and I badly wanted to go to these lessons with Lexi and claim another victory.

By the time the day of our meeting came, I could walk down the stairs and back up again, a new achievement. Now I knew they surely couldn't stop me from going to my Greek classes.

During the meeting, as a sign of defiance and togetherness and a show of love, Lexi and I held hands as we sat and looked around at everyone in the room. I now had my release date, which would be January 27 2014.

On the Tuesday evening when I was going to attend my Greek class, I was both excited and nervous that I was at last being allowed out by myself. I arranged for a taxi to pick me up from the Cherryburn, feeling nervous about the prospect of seeing my classmates again. I wasn't worried about my progress in the class as I believed I would be up to date, thanks to the homework I'd been doing.

I met Lexi outside the restaurant at 5.45 and she walked down the steps with me to have a drink before the class started at 6 pm – we both liked a glass of red wine. Everyone knew I was coming that evening. Anastasia, our teacher, was doing the lessons for pleasure as it was almost a hobby for her and a way of making a few bob, charging only £10 a lesson, so it was not seen as a professional class. With us were another couple, Stephen and Sandie. Having the class there was a good idea as afterwards we had free time to enjoy a meal there, ordering in Greek of course from the owners, Dimitros and Anna, which was good for our language building. I was doing well, having been dipping my toes into the language during my travels and Greek island hopping since 2000 and mainly using my Greek in restaurants and bars. The restaurant people were happy as Tuesday was a quiet night.

Best of all it was great to spend time with Lexi, having a meal and a drink together before she took me back to the stroke unit in time for my last medication of the day and lights out. The following morning I took great delight in telling everyone how well the evening had gone.

During that January of 2014 everything was starting to move rapidly, and I was making amazing progress in every area. I passed every test set by Ivy in the occupational therapy area sessions. My brain had successfully rewired itself; parts of it were now taking over from the parts whose function I had lost through the stroke. The human brain is amazing, and neurology is a fascinating subject. I was going to be leaving Cherryburn Unit in good shape. I felt I did not have the neurological problems that that most stroke victims are left with, which I had been determined would happen right from the start. I was a survivor – I had the power to fight back! I wanted my life back and I want to get back into society, and now I was nearly there. Victory was tantalisingly close.

I was going to be leaving under what is called the ERD or Early Release Date scheme. I could now wash and dress myself and was well enough to leave hospital, and I no longer needed a hospital bed. I still needed some care, but

I could have this at home, as I was going to be moved into an independent living facility unit, where I could feel I was once again part of society. I could enjoy my independent living and self-medicate, with tablets delivered to me each week. I would now receive physiotherapy at home from Sheila, a no-nonsense Irish woman who worked with the Cherryburn Stroke Unit under the EDR scheme. I would also be visited by an occupational therapist and a social worker, so one of the requirements for the building was an entrance with a buzzer and intercom so I could let in visitors. I also had to have the use of a lift, a walk-in shower and a kitchen suitable for me to work in, as I would be cooking for myself again. I was also going to be doing my own cleaning, with a care tram visiting me to see to anything I couldn't manage, like washing up my dishes and pots and mopping the kitchen and bathroom floors, all difficult with the use of only one hand. There would be three visits a day at first. It was financed by the NHS and Newcastle City Council and designed to get people back on their feet after lengthy spells in hospital.

For now though, and for the rest of my time in the stroke unit, I still had a lot of work to do. There were many 'exit meetings' with the specialists who had been looking after me to make sure I was going to be ready to be released.

An appointment was made for me to view my new home in St Cuthbert's Court in the Coxlodge area of Newcastle. I was taken there in a wheelchair taxi by Jenny and Ivy.

There I met Wendy and Margaret, who ran the place. They acted as wardens, although they were not on site 24 hours. As I was pushed along the corridors to my room, no. 69, a one-bedroom apartment, I decided I liked the feel of St Cuthbert's Court. Inside I was allowed to get out of my wheelchair and walk around. There were two big windows overlooking the garden, a small but fully-equipped modern kitchen with a small window overlooking the communal garden. St Cuthbert's had 40 apartments for people who, like myself, wanted independent living. Besides the communal garden there was a communal kitchen and lounge area where all the residents could meet up. I liked what I saw. I liked Wendy and Margaret, who seemed nice and easy to get on with.

Jenny and Ivy had to make sure I could get into the walk-in shower, and I found I could do so easily. They also had to make sure I could walk around the apartment safely, and made notes for when they reported back.

It was a fine sunny day, so I had time to look at the garden. Even though I liked everything I saw, I wanted to make a second visit – after all, this was going to be my new home. So another visit was arranged, which meant another trip out! This time I asked if I could take Lexi with me. If only we could be setting up our new home, our own little love nest. I doubt very much now that our dream of running off into the sunset to live on a Greek island had been taken away by the stroke, something else I had so cruelly lost, but for now she still seemed to be standing by me, and she joined Jenny, Ivy and me on my second visit to my new home. Lexi also liked what she saw and the set-up St Cuthbert's had to offer. My apartment would be furnished by Newcastle City Council under the ERD scheme, along with the NHS. No wonder the city councils and the Health Service don't have any money, financing this sort of thing! You never hear about good things like this about the public services – it's always doom and gloom.

I was going to work closely with a woman called Jo from Newcastle City Council, linked to the ERD scheme, to pick my furniture from a brochure. Only the prices were missing. And so I started picking the things I wanted for my new home.

Time was ticking on as I waited for January 27. I wasn't going to be able to walk out of the door by myself – I had to arrange for my friend David to take me to my new home in the wheelchair I had been given. In time I would gain enough strength to walk further and learn to cross roads again, but I could not do this until it had been agreed by Sharon, who would be helping me to do this on her home visits. I had to follow all these rules and guidelines under the scheme, so I still had battles to fight.

One of my last tasks was to make sure I could self-medicate, but after all I had been through this was going to be simple. I just had to take my tablets out of the pack on the right days at breakfast, lunch and bedtime.

During my exit meetings it was becoming clear that although I would be out of hospital, my life was not going to be my own. I wouldn't be allowed to do anything or go anywhere without permission. I felt I would be like a prisoner let out under licence. I also felt it would easier for everyone if I was just sitting in a chair and put in front of a TV with someone coming to check on me periodically. A representative of the care team, a man called Chris, came to see me and seemed surprised that I felt like this. He kept saying things like 'We can do that for you' and 'That's what we're here for'. After what seemed a lengthy meeting, it was agreed that a care team would visit me three times a day to help with anything I couldn't do, like washing up, which is very difficult with only one hand. Visits were arranged around mealtimes. I had already decided to keep to the mealtimes I had had at the stroke unit, as this worked fine. So my morning call was arranged for 8.30, lunch at 12.30 and teatime at 6.30. I didn't see the need for a late evening call as I could take myself to bed. Chris seemed surprised that I could take my own tablets, saying many stroke patients could not, and also needed help with showering and dressing. That was never going to be me!

I had the power to make sure I was going to get my life back, a new life, not a second life where I could put right any wrongs from a first life but a new life, a new way of living. I knew it was going to be difficult, but I had a chance and I was going to take it. Chris agreed that I would be taken out shopping to a supermarket once a week in my wheelchair by a member of the care team. There were two near me, an Asda and a Tesco, and both were suitable. I could walk, but nobody yet knew I far. This was going to be worked on during my home physio visits.

I told Chris his team only needed to help with the mopping of the kitchen and bathroom floors, very difficult to do with one arm. I wanted to do everything else myself, or at least try, including cleaning my flat, as I had lost none of my pride. I also believed that the work I had done in the OT sessions had helped with my neurological condition and keeping my brain active. My reading and my Greek language sessions had also helped.

Soon the big day came for my discharge. I did have mixed feelings about leaving; I badly wanted to get out of the place, but I knew I would miss everyone. I had a new life waiting for me, a new way of living. It was going to be difficult, as I would be on my own most of the time with no team of nurses at the end of a call button. Of course I did have Wendy and Margaret at St Cuthbert's Court to call on, and the care team would be visiting three times a day.

I was given one last check of my SATS, blood pressure, oxygen levels and temperature, and they were all perfect. I received my discharge wallet and my first week's medication in the medipack from Claire and we had a final chat about what lay ahead. I had time to say my goodbyes to all the wonderful staff before David came to pick me up. I wasn't able to walk out of the main doors as I would have liked of course – I had to leave in my wheelchair with him pushing. But I was leaving – something many patients would never get the chance to do.

Chapter 4

Finding my feet

Having paid my deposit and got the keys, I was at last able to move into my new home. All my new furniture had been delivered and Lexi had very kindly moved my personal belongings from my old flat.

My new home was full of boxes and bags of clothes and I had a lot of work to do getting everything straight. My first visitor was Lexi, bringing a coffee machine as a house-warming gift – she knew I liked my coffee. The machine was easy to use and only needed one hand, something Lexi had thought about. It felt so good to spend time with her in the privacy of my own home. Anyone seeing us would have known we were a young couple in love. It felt as if each new day had been created just for us. Our dream of running away together to a Greek island had cruelly been taken away from us, but if you keep asking 'Why me?' it would drive you crazy.

At St Cuthbert's Court I was able to walk from my apartment on the first floor along the corridor to the lift and down to the communal laundry room on the ground floor. I wanted to do my own laundry, but I would need the care team to help with changing my bedding once a week.

Lexi stayed with me for the rest of that Friday afternoon and we unpacked and tried out the coffee machine. She was back the next morning to take me shopping – my first shop since the stroke. I don't know what I would have done without her. We didn't talk about our lost dream of living on a Greek island, as this had hurt us both. However she seemed to be standing by me. She would pop round when she could and I would see her each week at the Greek class.

I did not know the area around my new home. Coxlodge was a new residential area near to Gosforth, Kenton and Kingston Park and not far from Newcastle Airport – I could see the control tower from the main road outside the building. Across the road was a small convenience store, a bookie's and a small café. They didn't seem far, but right now they were too far for me to walk to. Getting to them was going to be one of my goals.

I would be receiving an hour of home physio from Sheila from the stroke unit to continue the work I had been doing with Jenny, along with an occupational therapist and a social worker. I wasn't allowed to do anything until I was passed fit. Because of my neurological condition I would have something called 'inner retention'. Because the stroke had affected the right side of my brain, which controls the left side of the body, the theory was that I might forget to look left when crossing a road, so I had to learn to do this again. Sharon would help me to deal with this, and she would also help me to learn to handle money again. I didn't think this would be a problem, but I was told most stroke patients do lose this ability. But as I had reminded the specialists so many times, I wasn't like most stroke patients!

Sharon would also help me to learn how to catch a bus again, which I needed to do if I was to get my life back. For now, until I had passed all these tests, I wasn't allowed to do anything or go anywhere unless somebody came to pick me up.

Under this umbrella of care my door intercom buzzer was going to be kept busy! I made sure that apart from the care team I would only have one visitor per day. With my medication delivery on a Friday morning, I felt my buzzer would be the busiest in the building.

My good friend David popped back to see me over the weekend. Lexi did a big shop for me to fill my cupboards, which were empty, and left David and me to arrange the furniture the way I wanted it.

My first task was to make my new place feel like home. This meant spending time over the first week unpacking the boxes Lexi had so kindly packed for me. I had lots of things from my travels and my holidays in Greece, and felt this was chance to display them and give my flat a Greek theme throughout with my collection of mugs, one from each island I had visited, on top of my kitchen cupboards, my ornaments in the living area, which would also have a 'photo wall' covered in bright pictures and photographs of the blue seas and skies, giving the live are a bright colour scheme of blue and white, the colours of the Greek flag. My bedroom acquired a sunset theme with pictures of sunsets I had taken, making another photo wall. With my books arranged on the bookcases, I was really pleased with the outcome of my hard work.

Although this was independent living, I wasn't allowed to do anything outside until I had been assessed by Sharon. I was allowed to go to my Greek class without supervision, as I had been 'passed' to do this. I could now get in and out of a car safely and Lexi was always going to meet me outside the restaurant and bring me home after the class. Of course I had the steep wooden steps down to the restaurant to contend with, but over time I did master them, going down and back up them without Lexi helping me or even being beside me.

The next class soon came round the following Tuesday, and I found the number of a taxi firm which would take me.

It was my chance to enjoy a bit of freedom, have a glass of wine or two and enjoy a meal and quality time with Lexi.

There were only four of us in the class that week, the other two being Stephen and Sandie. In the restaurant, I felt back in society again, but the best thing was having time with Lexi.

I had started to meet the other residents of St Cuthbert's Court, usually as they sat out in the communal garden on a fine day having a natter, and there was always somebody in the communal laundry, again a great place for a chat. The two managers were about during the week, with both Wendy and Margaret in the office on a Wednesday. This became one of my favourite days, as I liked them both and got on well with them, often having a coffee together. My other favourite day was a Friday, when I heard Ashleigh's beautiful voice over the intercom announcing that she had brought my medication. I affectionately started calling her 'Tablet Woman'. Ashleigh was gorgeous, with a lovely figure to match her voice. I used to stand at the door so that I could see her gorgeous smile as she walked down the corridor. I would collect my tablets from her, then watch her cute backside as she walked back along the corridor. In time we started to get into conversation. 'Tablet Woman' did not realise that she had become an important part of my rehabilitation, as I looked forward so much to seeing her. We would become quite good friends during the two years I would spend at St Cuthbert's Court.

Everything was going well in my new independent life. I was getting stronger and looking after myself better and better, eating healthily. I felt it important that I should do my own shopping, not do it on line or give a list to someone. I would be taken out in my wheelchair on a Thursday morning by Lennon, the care worker assigned to me. I did notice that people treat you differently when you're in a wheelchair. They often don't see you, and speak to the person pushing the chair. When I asked a shop assistant for some marmalade she didn't reply to me but spoke to Lennon, saying 'What sort of marmalade?' I don't think people realise they are doing it – it probably comes down to training, which I would like to get involved now that I have experienced it.

Being able to choose what meat, vegetables etc I bought gave me the opportunity to plan my week and take control of my meals. This was important to me as it showed that I had lost none of my ability to plan things, again all part of my personal pride. I was told that most stroke patients lost the ability to do this, but yet again I was telling everyone that I wasn't going to be like most stroke patients!

Being out of hospital and away from illness and negativity, eating more healthily and being able to sit out in the communal gardens made all the difference. I could feel I was getting stronger, and my whole situation was improving rapidly. My home physio visits were going very well. I was working on going down the stairs at my flat rather than always using the lift, and often got a round of applause from the people in the communal lounge and kitchen. My stamina was improving and my walking was getting stronger, steadier and safer. With everything going so well, Sheila and I agreed a set of goals or markers to see how far I could walk, the end goal being to walk over to the shops across the road. Sharon also helped me to make sure I could cross the road safely and handle my money in the shops. If I passed these tests it would open up a whole new world!

In fact I achieved this fairly quickly and soon ticked off the list of things I had wanted to do on my own. Oh the carrot of a Saturday football bet, and what it can make you achieve!

Over my two years at St Cuthbert's Court I made very good friends with the people who ran the three units over the road, in particular Joanie and Den in the café, which was called 'Luv Ur Grub'. On a Saturday morning after my care call, I would first collect my newspaper from the convenience store to work out a football bet, then to the café, where I would have a full English cooked breakfast, sitting outside if it was nice enough. Den would kindly put a table and chair outside for me and I would eat a delicious breakfast while reading and sorting out my football bet. I was not getting my independence back and feeling very much part of society once again. I could now visit the store to get a paper, top up my mobile phone, have a go in the

Lottery or buy anything I needed which had been omitted from the weekly shop.

Because I was doing so well, Sharon told me I was ready for the next phase – an outing with her. We were going to catch a bus into the city centre, go shopping and have a coffee in one of the many coffee shops. I would learn important tasks such as catching a bus, getting off at the right stop, dealing with money, walking along busy streets and making decisions about what shops to go to. Sharon would be observing me and recording everything. I thought it would feel a bit like taking a driving test. I would be leading the trip, deciding what shops to go into. As it happened I needed a new laundry basket, one that would be easier for me to carry from my flat to the laundry room, so this would be my test. Going into town without supervision would open up a whole new world to me, as I would be able to meet friends for a coffee or simply just pop into town myself and people-watch.

I passed every test with Sharon, having no problems handling money when buying my laundry basket and then treating her to a coffee. Getting the bus, even finding a seat on the busy moving bus, caused no problems, and nor did paying the driver. Next in this phase we were going on another trip and catching a train on the Tyne and Wear Metro system running from the centre of Newcastle out to Sunderland, the coast and the airport. I also passed this assessment, so I was now free to go out by myself during the day. Above all I felt that I was now gaining control of my life and not being controlled by the authorities. I really wanted my life back on my terms. I knew my old life had been cruelly taken away, but I wanted to get as close to it as possible. What a comeback, what a story it would make!

As 2014 went on I started going out more, going into town on the bus or visiting a retail park at Kingston Park. When I did my weekly shop with Lennon at Tesco, I would still be in my wheelchair, until I was told otherwise. I started buying my own clothes again, at Matalan in the retail park. By March 2014 I was able to walk a good distance and I asked Sheila and Sharon about coming out of the wheelchair and giving it back to the NHS Trust. The weather was now getting better, which meant I could sit outside more in the communal garden. The garden was one of the things that had appealed to me on my initial visits to St Cuthbert's. I was able to enjoy the early spring sunshine and felt much better sitting outside in the sun than staying in my flat, however much I liked it. I was getting to know many of the other residents and often the same small group would sit outside in the daytime, when it was fine. Most of the apartments were one-bedroomed like mine and had just one occupant. There were a couple of two-bedroom flats and two three-bedroom ones, one of which was occupied by a couple called Eric and Christine, who needed the extra room because they both played guitar, and occasionally we could hear the sound of them practising.

Eric was undergoing his own rehabilitation following a hip replacement, and they both liked to sit outside, though sometimes it was just me out there enjoying the peace and quiet.

The patio area didn't get the sun until 10 am, but I soon realised that I could go across the road to the café, where Den would put out a table and chair for me and I could enjoy a coffee with my breakfast. The sun shone on this area from 8 am, but I couldn't get over there until after my morning call by the care team.

When I went into town I found more places where I could sit in the sun, outside a coffee shop on busy Northumberland Street or outside a bar near Eldon Square shopping centre opposite the market. The mezze bar was great for watching the world go by. I was beginning to feel good about life again and enjoying the simple things we all take for granted, like sitting in the sun. More of my old self was coming back. I had lost some of my character and personality after the stroke and had gone into my shell like a hermit crab, but it was returning.

One afternoon while sitting in the garden I had my own 'eureka' moment. I wanted some proper hot sunshine. I wanted to see the blue sky that was on all the pictures I had on display in the flat. That Mediterranean dream was still nagging inside me. I wanted to travel again! And after what I had been through, I felt I deserved a holiday. I believe the early work I did with Ivy in the stroke unit was a major factor in my regaining my independence, along with my determination to read books even though it hurt my eyes after a short time.

I knew I would have a battle on my hands when I said I wanted to take a holiday, as I would have to get permission from the ERD scheme. I had won so many battles already, but I knew there would be many more ahead. If I went on holiday it would not be in a wheelchair!

I told my social worker and clinical psychologist about my plans, and they looked at me as if I had two heads! They both told me it wasn't going to be as easy as that. I couldn't just go off and book a holiday. Yes, I was doing well in my independent living, but I was still under the umbrella of the care scheme and I would have to get permission from all the people involved to even have a chance of getting away on holiday, and certainly not on my own. So the answer from these two was to forget it, at least for now.

I had the money to finance a holiday as I was still on full sick pay and as I was not going out drinking and socialising my bank account did look healthy. I was given a list of people I would have to get permission from, the first being the stroke team who were overseeing the whole operation of the ERD scheme. I would have to convince Hilary, and the next two would be the two doctors I was still under at the RVI. As it happened I was due to see them in March for a full check-up following my release. This was another trip out in a taxi ambulance. This seemed the perfect time to talk to Dr Irvine, my cardiologist, and Dr Luwe, my stroke doctor, so I could get their professional opinion and their thoughts about my plan to go on holiday.

I felt comfortable in the medical room as Dr Irvine conducted his tests. The first was an Echo scan, and this came back clear with my heart chambers and valves all looking good. I was then wired to an ECG machine, and this too came back fine, with a perfect regular heartbeat.

Dr Irvine asked me if I had any questions. 'I want to go on holiday,' I said.

'Follow me,' he said. He signalled to the nurse and she pushed me into a room which looked like his office. The nurse had taken my blood pressure and temperature, and both had come back perfect. I had been looking after myself since leaving the stroke unit.

In his office, Dr Irvine took on the aura of a detective about to conduct an interview. He sat behind his desk with cold, steely blue eyes fixed on me. Finally he spoke.

'Young man, this puts me and everyone here in a difficult situation,' he said. 'It's not something we usually get from a stroke patient, and frankly I am not happy about it.' I reminded him that I had become a stroke survivor, and I wanted my life back. There was a pause, and then he started to speak again, firing short sentences at me. 'What if you had a fall? Have you really thought this through? How are you going to manage? What I you can't get on the aircraft? We would have to assess you using the aircraft steps. What if you need help? What if something happened to you on holiday when you were on your own? You can't expect to fly three months after a stroke.'

So many what ifs! First I reminded him that I had passed the three-month mark. I told him that I had thought about it and I would not be doing anything adventurous. I wouldn't be going island hopping – I just wanted a week in the sun, to find a beach and relax. All I would be doing was relaxing in the sun by the pool or on the beach. I would find a flight from Newcastle Airport and stay in a hotel where my bed would be made, no cleaning, all my meals cooked for me. But he was taking some convincing. 'What if you can't get off the lounger? What if you can't walk on sand because of your weakness in your left leg?' Those two wretched words again – what if!

At the time it felt as if I was going to be arrested and charged with a horrific crime I had not committed. After another long pause he said, 'In my professional opinion, I think it's the wrong thing to do. However I can't stop you, I can only advise you. The answer is a no from me. David, you have to remember that you've had a life-changing experience, and you are not the same person you were. However I can see this is what you want, and you are doing so well that I can't stop you.' I thought he had finished, but then he went on: 'Dr Luwe knows you better than me. You are going to see him today. We'll see what his opinion is.'

This was a big blow to my holiday plans, but there was

hope. I knew Dr Luwe and had built up a good rapport with him. So off I went to another part of the hospital to see him.

Dr Luwe didn't sit behind a desk. Instead he sat next to me and put me through a short series of exercises such as standing up, getting out of my chair, walking around it and then sitting back down again. 'Excellent, young man!' he said when I'd done them, clapping his hands. I felt at ease straight away in his company. There were more tests as he went on to check my reflexes, hitting me with a small medical hammer on both knees and elbows. Importantly, he was testing how I would respond on my left side compared to the right. He also tested me on the sensations of hot and cold and sharp or blunt instruments. Then he measured my height and weight. Finally he went and sat at his desk, working on his PC and no doubt checking my records.

Finally he turned round to speak to me again. 'I'm very pleased with your progress and I'm happy with the reports from Sharon [my OT] on your outings. This is very positive, David. I'm very pleased with your progress. Very well done, my boy!'

This had been a much more relaxed session than the one with Dr Irvine.

'OK, here's the score' he said finally. 'I told you it's my experience that you could beat this. Nothing has happened to change my mind. There is no need for you to come back here for any more visits, wasting my time and yours. I will get Sheila to monitor your blood pressure. Do you have any questions?'

Now was my chance. I said, 'Yes, I want to go on holiday, but apparently I need your permission.'

'Permission is a strong word,' he said. 'You need my advice. As you are under the umbrella of our care, your welfare and health are our concern. This does put me in a difficult position, as we don't normally get stroke patients wanting to go off on holiday. But you are doing so well so far. I don't want you to be taking risks or to have any setbacks. Remember another stroke could kill you, or leave you with a severe disability. Is it worth the risk? What if something happened?' He paused for a moment. 'I do remember your love of the sun and the Greek islands. Where and when would you go? Who would you go with?'

'I was thinking of going as soon as possible, maybe in May,' I replied. 'This means Rhodes, Kos or Crete, or even Cyprus. I would be going on my own and booking the holiday through a travel agent.'

'What about that nice young lady who visited you in the Cherryburn?' he asked. I told him that wasn't possible, no matter how much I would have liked it. Lexi was still with her partner. The stroke had put an end to our dream of running away to the sun.

Dr Luwe did agree that the sun would be good for me as I would get the sun on my body and in my bones and soak up vitamin D. He went on, 'Remember, I don't want any mishaps. You are doing so well. Remember how you got here today, and how you are getting home – in a wheelchair taxi.' He was gently reminding me that I was still being pushed around in a wheelchair. I would not be going on holiday in one – in fact I was determined to get rid of the bloody thing before I went on my holiday, to prove to everyone that I could do it.

'The problem with younger stroke patients is that they all think they can run before they can walk,' said Dr Luwe.

'I would have full control of the holiday and have the choice of where I go and when,' I told him. 'I would choose a flight time to suit me and take my medication from Newcastle Airport.'

With that I thought I had clinched the deal. Dr Luwe then said, 'OK, here's the score. When you book the holiday I want you to take Sharon with you. I would feel more comfortable with that as she would advise you and make sure you are going on the right holiday for your needs. I'll contact her to let her know.'

I agreed to this as I felt this would be meeting him halfway. After all I certainly wouldn't be going on a Club 18-30 holiday! Not that I could at the age of 49.

Dr Luwe said he would ring Sharon and set it up, and also contacting Hilary, who was in charge of the stroke unit. Then he stood up and shook my hand. 'Goodbye David, I wish you luck in life,' he said. 'Remember what I've told you as this is your last visit to us.' I would miss Dr Luwe. As I got to the door he shouted, 'Enjoy your holiday, and don't forget to send me a postcard!'

We parted with laughter and smiles as the ambulance taxi crew began to push me back down to the main entrance and the waiting ambulance taxi. My hospital days were now behind me. I felt very good about myself and within myself, so much so that I wanted to wave to everyone I passed by, like the Pope in his Popemobile. I had given a good account of myself at the hospital. However I was sure I had heard nagging doubt in both doctors' voices, even though they had both given me permission to go on holiday. I'm sure they were ready to say 'I told you so' if anything went wrong. I was now even more determined to prove to them, and everybody else, that I was a stroke survivor and could still do things I wanted. Everybody has the power to change their life, given the chance.

And things were going to change once I got home. First I would get stronger, with the help of my home physio sessions with Sheila, by getting her help to use the stairs even though I could use the lift. This would increase my stamina and strength. I decided to ring the stroke unit to come and take away my wheelchair – I wasn't going to use it! I would be going shopping with Lennon without it. I would push my own trolley around the supermarket, filling up the trolley myself. I was going to show them! Lennon's only job (apart from driving) would be to empty the trolley onto the conveyor belt and pack my goods for me. I knew that after my holiday in the sun I would come back a different and stronger person. This was me fighting back.

It was now the end of March, and I had been out of the stroke unit and in my new home for two months. Things were going very well in my independent living. I was cooking for myself most nights of the week – only Tuesday was different, as that was the night I had dinner at Simply Greek. I didn't have the confidence to go out by myself to the pub or into town as my left arm lay across my chest, which would make people think there was something wrong with me. That was something I would have to deal with. I thought the holiday would help with this as I would be around people I didn't know anything about me or my situation. I hoped the holiday would bring me out of my shell.

But on the last Tuesday in March, Anastasia dropped a bombshell. She told us that in June she would be going back to live in Athens. She told us she would continue the classes until she left, but after that everything was going to change. The four of us were stunned. We had all so enjoyed having our lessons and then sharing a meal with wine. I would probably miss it most, as it was my only night out and I had come to feel very comfortable in the surroundings of the restaurant.

We all wanted to continue learning Greek, so we knew we would have to find an alternative. Lexi and I had met, fallen in love and shared our dream of going off to live on a small Greek island and live happily ever after. But the stroke had put an end to that. The other couple, Stephen and Sandra, had their own dream of going to live in Greece, in the Peloponnese.

It took a while, but finally we did find an alternative, at Newcastle Language Centre in Eldon Square. This would be an official class, and it would be more formal and more expensive as we would be paying for a classroom and a teacher. It was still on Tuesday evenings though, so I wouldn't have to change any care calls. We all signed up for the new class to start at the beginning of the new term in September, paying £300 each for the ten lessons.

Dr Luwe had kept his word and contacted Hilary, the woman in charge of the stroke team. She thought it was a good idea to take Sharon, my occupational therapist, with me when I booked the holiday, as part of my early rehabilitation and learning to do everything for myself again. I was now taking control of these trips with Sharon, who would call at my apartment before we went out and come back home with me afterwards to complete a report. These trips were easier now I no longer had a lunchtime care call.

Even though everyone now seemed to be going along with my holiday idea, I still felt none of them were 100 per cent behind me. Looking back on it Hilary did make a good point – how could I be assessed going up and down aircraft steps? The only option she came up with me was working on this and then being assessed on the stairs at home. I felt sure they would all have preferred to stick me in a wheelchair and sit me in front of the TV all day – easier for them! Yes, I knew they were risks, but taking risks is part of life.

So in the first week of April I went into Newcastle city centre with Sharon. I had chosen to go to Thomas Cook and to book a one-week holiday in May. I could go on any day in any week to fit in with everyone. I would be able to fly directly to my chosen island, which could be Crete, Rhodes, Cyprus or Kos, all of which I had been to before. I had always been organised before the stroke, and I wanted to prove to everyone, and to myself, that I still was. This was about more than just a holiday!

We walked into Thomas Cook and approached the desk of a travel advisor called Lisa, who looked nice and friendly. We sat down and I explained what had happened to me and where I wanted to go, then introduced Sharon, who explained what she was there for. Lisa started typing on her keyboard, eyes locked on the computer screen. She asked me if I used any sort of walking aid – no. Did I require special assistance at the airport or boarding/leaving the aircraft? This meant using the ambi-lift to board the plane. Sharon replied, 'Yes he does want special assistance'. I explained to Lisa that I didn't, as I wanted this trip to be as normal as possible for me, and also I wanted to find out just what I could do. If I had the assistance, which is provided free by most airports, I wouldn't know what I was capable of achieving. Again those two little words 'what if' came up.

She said I should take up the offer in case something went wrong. I explained to Lisa that this was my holiday, on my terms, and I wanted to be on control.

Lisa asked what sort of board I was looking for. It was agreed that the all-inclusive option was the best for me, as it meant everything would be provided by the hotel. I agreed to this, even though I had not chosen this option before as it gave you no chance of venturing out of the hotel to see the resort or spend money within the local economy. I had always previous travelled independently, getting a flight to Athens then making my way to the port of Piraeus to catch a ferry to start an island-hopping adventure around the Greek islands. My best adventure had been in 2008, when I had spent six months going around the islands – 'my Aegean summer' as I called it.

Lisa came up with a week in Cyprus, flying at either 0700 or 2300 on May 7. I chose the earlier flight as the journey would suit my medication times. I also had to consider the return journey a week later, and the option I chose here was at 1445 from Larnaca. I would land back in Newcastle at 1800. Sharon seemed bemused as I explained my choice and the reasons for it. Lisa looked impressed, as once again I was proving that there was nothing wrong with my ability to plan, make decisions and solve problems.

I would be staying in the Hotel Constantinos the Great, a big beach hotel in the resort of Protaras. It looked fabulous, a five-star hotel on the beach on three floors with two lifts and suitable for guests in wheelchairs. Lisa had done a brilliant job. I was very happy, and so was Sharon, as it fitted all her professional requirements. Again because I wanted this holiday to be as normal as possible, I chose a coach transfer from the airport to the hotel with the other passengers. This would take around 45 minutes after a five-hour flight. I could have opted for a private taxi transfer, but that was too easy. The steps up into the coach would be a new challenge for me, as the buses and coaches I was using on my trips out at home all had low-level doors and flooring.

You have to buy travel insurance when you book any holiday, and I purchased the Thomas Cook Gold Travel option. Having declared that I had had a stroke, I would have to buy extra insurance called 'pre-existing health insurance'. This would cover me against anything connected with my stroke if anything went wrong during my holiday, which would keep the 'what if' parties happy. Lisa had booked everything else, but I would have to do this myself on the phone.

I felt great having booked and paid for my 'luxury holiday', as Sharon called it. Time to celebrate, so I said I'd take her for a coffee at Costa Coffee, a short walk away. This was a chance to go through the itinerary Lisa had give me. Sharon still felt I should have taken the special assistance, so we agreed to disagree. It certainly felt that exciting times were ahead. I now had something to look forward other than Tablet Woman's Friday visits!

With all the excitement I had to remind myself that I had only been out of the Cherryburn Stroke Unit for two months. I had come a long way, but it was still early days in my rehabilitation and I still had a very long way to go. I was getting my life back, but it was important for me to keep my feet on the ground, remain focused and not get too carried away by the success I was having and how well I was doing.

Sharon had reported back to the teams of people involved in the ERD scheme, and most of them felt I should have taken the help on offer from the airlines and the airport. But I was taking my holiday my way, and I was determined to prove everybody wrong. I knew I had a lot of work to do before the holiday – I needed to shop for clothes and buy a new trolley case which I could pull along with me. With only a month to organise everything, my first task was to ring up about my medical insurance. I would have to go through a medical screening over the phone to determine how much cover I needed and how much I would have to pay – Lisa had explained everything. I would also have to declare all my medication to the insurance company and the airline. The week's worth of medication I would be taking with me would go in my hand luggage. I would need to tell the pharmacy about my holiday. As I would be away on the Friday, Tablet Woman would have to deliver two weeks' worth of medication on the previous Friday. I would also need to contact my care team about stopping my calls for that week and organising a couple of extra shopping calls, so I could buy a new holiday wardrobe and that new case. It would be easier to go with them in a car. I was allowed to have extra trips and calls as long as the management of the care team agreed and had the carers and time to arrange them. I would go the big Matalan store at Kingston Park, where I knew I could get everything under one roof. It was a good trip out for me, and it gave me time to sit and rest over a coffee people-watching. This sort of trip made me feel part of society again.

When I rang about the extra medical insurance it came to only £52, a lot less than I had expected. I was now covered against anything happening in connection with the stroke.

With so much to organise, my social worker kindly offered to help, but I declined as I wanted to do myself for two reasons. First I wanted to show everyone that I could still plan, and secondly I felt it was part of the excitement of the build-up to the holiday. I still had three weeks to go if I followed my dad's philosophy, the six Ps – Perfect Planning Prevents Piss-Poor Performance. I was all set. I wasn't sure what the week away would hold or how it would change the direction of my life, but I knew it would.

Me (left) with my father and brother, taken before the stroke

A postcard for the Constantinos the Great Hotel, where my adventure in Cyprus began

Another view of the Constantinos the Great Hotel

The view from my room at the hotel

With Michela, my princess

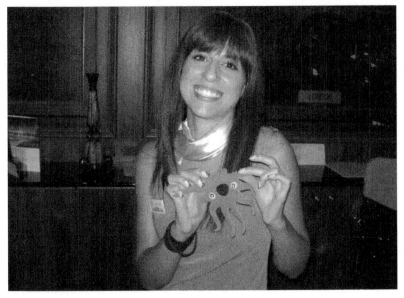

Maria with the toy octopus I gave her

With bubbly Chelsea

With my friend Mr Stathis, the hotel manager

Chapter 5

Cyprus

When the morning of May 7 arrived, I was up very early, at 3 am. I had never seen St Cuthbert's Court so quiet. My taxi was booked for 4 am for the short journey to Newcastle Airport 40 minutes away. I wanted to get there early to avoid any queues at the check-in – everyone knows that it's when you've dropped your luggage at the check-in that a holiday begins. I would take my morning medication at the airport while having breakfast at one of the many eateries. I was determined to keep my tablet times as close to my routine as possible.

My early arrival at the airport worked well and everything went smoothly, with no queue at the check-in desks – in fact I was the only one there. Being early also meant I could choose my seat. I asked for an aisle seat on the right so I could move around and stretch my left leg out if I needed to. This would stop any concerns about developing DVT (deep vein thrombosis).

I was surprised how busy the departure lounge and airside areas were. Checking the departure screens, a lot of flights were taking off around the same time as mine.

As I walked up the aircraft steps I wanted to look around to savour what was happening and take in my achievement. After all it was less than two months since I had stopped using a wheelchair, and only four months since I had left the stroke unit, and here I was off on holiday on my own and about to board a plane under my own steam with all the other passengers.

The five-hour flight went well and didn't seem to take that long. The rest of the journey out went well too, including collecting my case from the luggage belt at Larnaca. My first job after collecting my case was to let Lexi know I had arrived safely. There was some confusion at the airport, as after clearing security and making my way out into the arrivals hall where all the holiday reps were waiting I found that even though I was on a Thomas Cook flight and booked through Thomas Cook, I had now somehow joined a First Choice holiday. It seemed I had been put on the wrong coach amongst the ones that were taking holidaymakers to their resorts and hotels. I could tell something was wrong when the rep was doing her head count. Anton, who worked for First Choice, sorted it out. He said he would be my rep at the hotel.

My fears about getting on and off the coaches came to the fore, as I then had to be taken off that coach and put onto the right one. It was a hot afternoon with a temperature of 40 degrees, and I was glad to finally sit down on the right coach. Anton and I would become good friends, even if he had put me on the wrong coach! He didn't travel with us on the coach as he was on airport duties that day – a member of the First Choice transfer team did that.

When we pulled up outside the Constantinos the Great Hotel, I was the only one to get off. I walked into the hotel entrance pulling my trolley case. It was very impressive, with two glass-walled lifts opposite the entrance doors so you could see the walkways of the three floors where the rooms were. I must have looked tired after my long journey, and I certainly felt it. It was now 3.30 pm Cyprus time – they are two hours ahead of the UK.

I had just put my case down to take in the scene in the hotel and savour my achievement when I heard a sweet voice say, 'Is everything all right sir?' It was a pretty girl on the reception desk with neat dark hair and a beautiful smile. I went over to the desk to check in and hand over my passport. The girl, whose name was Michela, had gorgeous hazel-brown eyes, and there was something very special about that smile. For a moment I stood transfixed, gazing into those beautiful eyes. I thought my days of getting a smile like that from a pretty girl had long gone. I wanted to say something, anything, but my throat had gone dry. But somehow I knew it would be fine for the week ahead.

'Welcome to the Constantinos,' she said. She handed me my room key, actually a card about the size of a credit card. My room was no 259 on the second floor. I followed as the day porter, Elias, took my case to my room. Like all the rooms in the hotel, no. 259 had stunning views of the Mediterranean. My side of the hotel was also overlooking the pool and terrace area with all the sun loungers.

I sat on my balcony in the heat, taking in the views and reading the information Michela had given me, including meal times and other information. Dinner was served at 7 pm in the main restaurant, so there would be plenty of time to unpack before going for a drink in the main bar. I hoped this holiday would give me back the confidence to be seen in bars and pubs again, the confidence I had lost after my stroke. Although my independent living was coming on very well, one thing I hadn't yet started doing was to go out in the evening (except for the Tuesday Greek evenings of course), preferring to stay in my flat and watch TV in the comfort and privacy of my home, lying in the big reclining chair I had bought myself. I was aware that I was now different from everyone else, with my left arm lying useless across my chest and having to hobble awkwardly about. I had always enjoyed a good social life and I was missing it.

I knew that I had lost the confidence to walk into a bar, feeling that people would be looking at me. But I had just been chatting to a complete stranger, the beautiful girl on reception, so maybe this holiday would be good for me ways in more ways than one.

It was while I was unpacking that I encountered my first problem. I had brought a new toothbrush, which was sealed inside one of those blister packs that everyone struggles to open. I hadn't brought the scissors I used to open everything in my home, so with no care team to help me this was one of those 'what if' moments people had been warning me about. I had to think what to do, and I came up with a solution. I plucked up the courage to ask the pretty girl on reception to help. I explained what I wanted and she smiled and said, 'If you need anything during your stay, you only have to ask me'. From this moment we started to build a good relationship. It also felt very comforting to know I had someone to turn to if I needed help, and more importantly, that the visible effects of the stroke didn't seem to bother her. Michela saw beyond the stroke – she saw me for the person I was. After what I had been through that made me feel good about myself.

It wasn't long before I encountered my second problem – taking a shower. At home I had a walk-in shower, but here I would to step into and out of the bath to take one. I hadn't thought about that. Suddenly I felt very vulnerable. I didn't remember this coming up in any of the conversations I had

had with any of the specialists. Suddenly all the 'what ifs' were going through my mind. Was everybody right about coming on holiday too soon?

Michela couldn't help me with this problem. I took a moment to step back and think about it, as Jenny and Ivy had taught me to do when faced with a problem.

I looked around. There was a towel rail on the wall which I could hold onto as I stepped in and out of the bath. I was stronger now – surely I could do this. I had to! My reputation was on the line. I remembered I was here to prove everybody wrong. If I wanted to see Michela again, I would have to do it. All these thoughts were spinning around in my head and my heart was pumping away.

I tried to get into the bath, holding onto the towel rail. I put my left leg in first, keeping my right leg on the bathroom floor. I had done it – with ease, in fact. I was ready for that drink at the bar.

Making my way from my room down to the bar, I passed by the reception desk. Just a glimpse of Michela's smile of warmth and beauty would give me a floating feeling. Our eyes would always meet and lock onto each other's gaze. I'm surprised I didn't bump into another guest, as I could never look where I was going when she was in my field of vision.

I had a drink in the lobby bar before dinner, and there I met Paniyotis, the head barman. Because of my medication I was allowed to drink only red wine – six o'clock had become 'red wine time' for me. I sat on a stool at the bar, to give myself the best chance of meeting other people and getting into conversation, but also so that I could see Michela in reception. During the week the staff in the main restaurant, the Emperor Restaurant, especially Miranda and Viktoria, were wonderful with me, being very attentive but never drawing attention to me. The waiting staff were mostly gorgeous young women who would help me to fetch my meals and carry my plate back to my table – it was an eat-as-much-as-you-like system. Miranda and Viktoria would cut up my meat for me, something I struggled with. They were a credit to the hotel, as were all the staff. I was being very well looked after and fussed over, and I liked it! I could feel that they were looking beyond the stroke and its effects and were seeing me for the person I was. I felt just like another guest.

My first night in the hotel was an early one, after I had made a phone call to Lexi. It had been a long day and I would be up early the next morning, eager to start catching the sun on a lounger by the pool. I had already chosen one from my balcony, one which was not too far from the pool bar, which served cold drinks all day. I would also have my welcome meeting in the hotel with Anton, the First Choice holiday rep. I made sure to say goodnight and thank you to Michela, who was finishing work at 11 and starting the next day at 3 pm.

As it turned out, for the first two days of my holiday

I didn't see the sun at all, as Cyprus was hit by two days of thunderstorms and heavy rain! So much for getting the sun on my body and into my bones. I can remember thinking, 'what have I done?' Lexi was concerned, and we were exchanging plenty of text messages – I wasn't sure if she was missing me or worried about me, or both.

Breakfast was served from 7-10 am each morning in the restaurant downstairs, which had views looking out to sea over the pool area. The hot food was again all set out in steel drums, while Greek yoghurt with fruit and honey was also available on the cold counters, and again you could take as much as you wanted. I opted for the yoghurt with fruit and honey, washed down with orange juice and coffee. The coffee you might have to get yourself from a machine, depending on how many staff were on duty in the breakfast room. Coffee would sometimes be served at your table by a waitress with a trolley. It was here I met Krisztina, a lovely waitress who seemed to take a shine to me, and I took a shine to her. She became known as my 'coffee woman', as she served me each morning so that I didn't have to fetch my own coffee. I had a table next to the window with views out to sea and the terraced area where around the pool, but looking out at pouring rain wasn't exactly what I had had in mind. I was unable to go outside, so after the welcome meeting with Anton I passed the morning looking around this impressive hotel. It was good to see him again. We were only just into my first full day and the list of people I had got to know was growing, including Sheri, who worked in the little shop tucked away in the corner of the lobby area. Sheri was English and supported Yeovil, who were in League Division Two like my team, Mansfield, so that led to lots of banter.

With the rain pouring down outside it gave me a chance to chat up Michela once she had started her shift in the afternoon. She remained professional of course, saying 'Excuse me sir' each time she needed to attend to another guest who needed help. I used my Greek on her to try to impress her, and she was impressed that I had learned some of her language. She started to teach me more words and phrases, and put me right when I got something wrong. I enjoyed having this sexy, beautiful young teacher, even if she was a hard taskmaster! The rain outside no longer mattered. She was enjoying this too and asked what had happened to me.

On the Saturday morning I awoke to a beautiful clear blue sky – the clouds had cleared at last and the little birdies were happily chirping away in the sun as I had coffee on my balcony. The Mediterranean was like a sheet of blue glass.

During those first few days I had plenty of contact with Lexi back home in Newcastle. I think she was missing me or worried about me, but whichever it was I had great delight sending a text message about the change in the weather. What I wanted now was a full day in the sun. The lounger I had picked out on the first day was vacant, so I made it mine. It felt good to feel the sun on my body and soak up the vitamin D. Summer had arrived in Cyprus. The weather stayed hot and sunny for the rest of the week, and I noticed how very relaxed the hotel felt. The staff and everyone who booked into the hotel seemed to be happy in their work and enjoying what they did. It was managed by Stathis Constantinou, or Mr Stathis as he was known – in Greece they don't use your surname, so I was Mr David.

Mr Stathis became a good friend as I got to know him. As a boss he was very well liked and the staff enjoyed working for him. It all added up to a happy ship. I was also getting to know lots of the staff, who all became my friends during the week as they got to know me.

The lounger I had chosen worked well, being so near the pool bar, as I drank plenty during the week in the heat of the Greek sun – water of course, with lemon or orange squash and ice. The staff, being so helpful, brought my drinks to me. Often they were brought by Eric, a Dutch member of the entertainment/animations team. He supported Ajax in Amsterdam and had heard of the Mansfield team, mainly thanks to our CEO, Carolyn Radford, so we had plenty of conversations about football. I was having no trouble getting safely on and off my lounger, which was another victory for me over the 'what if' club. I was also fine stepping into and out of the bath to have a shower every night; each time I did this it was becoming easier, so much so in fact that I no longer had to think about it.

People had noticed how much time I was spending talking to Michela and I was getting plenty of comments from other members of staff that if I wasn't on my lounger, people knew where to find me! We got on so very well. I loved the smiles she gave me whenever I passed reception. I loved the smiles she gave me when I was practising my Greek with her and she would formulate a sentence which I had to say to her. Even if I got it wrong she would smile at me with those gorgeous green eyes and make me say it again! She was a real taskmaster, but a beautiful one. Just being around her made me feel so good that it made me forget for a time what had happened to me. It was the first time I had been able to feel like that.

But then as my holiday was coming to an end, she delivered a devastating blow. My last full day was the Tuesday, and this was her day off! By the time she returned to work at 3 pm on the Wednesday, I would be on my way home. I would have to say goodbye on the Monday evening. But I wasn't going to think about that yet – I wanted to enjoy the time I still had with her.

I decided to get Mr Andreas, who was in charge of reception, to take a picture of us together on my camera. I liked Andreas; he made many comments about how much time I spent at the reception desk and would make fun of me, saying I spent more time there than he did! It was all good light-hearted banter. I was going to miss her and the way I felt so good about myself when I was with her, so much so that I could feel there was nothing wrong with me.

I had notice during the week how much more flexible my body felt. My walking especially felt so much smoother and more fluent. The holiday had been everything I had hoped for and much more. I had been socialising at the bar at red wine time, though not staying up late. I had got the confidence back to sit at a bar and not worry about what people thought of me. My left arm had become straighter and was no longer lying across my chest as it had before. I felt so much stronger after my week in the sun, and more importantly I felt so much better in myself and the way I saw the world. I wasn't angry at the world now about what had happened to me, just determined to keep on fighting back. Michela had shown me what a wonderful world we have around us and had told me in one of our many conversations that bad things make us stronger, and also 'It's not what happens to us in our lives that defines us, it's how we react to them'. She was so right! Things were going to be different once I got home, and all because a smile of such warmth and beauty from a pretty girl had changed everything.

I did get my photograph with Michela on the Monday. It was priceless to be able to put my arm round her and hold her in a goodbye hug on the Monday evening before she finished work. I got the impression she was very comfortable having my arm around her. Saying goodbye felt so difficult, but it was a majestic moment.

I still had one more full day left of this super holiday, and did my best to enjoy it in the sun on my lounger. But it was difficult, knowing I was going to be leaving tomorrow. Where had the week gone? It was strange having one last red wine session at the bar that evening, looking over to reception and not seeing Michela. I would now have to say my goodbyes to the girls in the restaurant who had done so much to help me through the week. Viktoria, from Moldova, had taken the biggest shine to me. But after my week in the hotel I had become a much stronger person. I didn't feel I was just leaving a hotel, but somewhere that had become very special. I had felt so at home here. I shook hands with everyone and even had a hug from Paniyotis.

I was up early on the Wednesday to have a last coffee on my balcony while taking in the wonderful views of the Mediterranean, which again looked like a sheet of blue glass, and listening to the little birds chirping away. That was a sound I hadn't appreciated before, but I certainly did now after my week in Cyprus. I was already looking at the world very differently as I recovered from my devastating near-fatal stroke, even more so after my week at the Constantinos the Great and meeting so many wonderful people. Michela had helped to teach me what a wonderful world we live in. Human life can feel fragile at times, but no matter what happens to us in our lives, when bad things happen they just make us stronger.

Following breakfast at 7 and taking my medication, I did my packing, with help from Janet, a guest I had got speaking to, as I was struggling with one hand to roll and fold my clothes tightly enough to get them into my case. I had had help on departure from Barry, one of the care team. I did intend just to throw my clothes into the case, as they would be going in the wash tomorrow, but Janet said it would keep them in better condition if they were rolled or folded.

I felt I was going back a stronger person than I had been a week ago, better mentally and physically, but would anyone else notice? In any case, after a wonderful week which I knew would change the direction of my life, I felt in control of myself once more for the first time since the stroke.

I spent the morning saying my goodbyes to everyone in the hotel before my 11.15 pick-up for Larnaca Airport and the flight home. But this was beginning to feel like leaving home, not going home; I felt I belonged in Cyprus. Even so the flight home was enjoyable, as was my time in the airport, having one last 'red wine time'. It was on the flight home that something suddenly occurred to me – I was going to leave a card for Michela telling her how she made me feel, but I hadn't got round to doing it. I don't think it was because I had chickened out; perhaps subconsciously

I had done it on purpose so that I would have to go back some time to say how I felt. I would have said thank you for the help she had given me and how she made me feel, and what I thought about her. For now though, it would be back to independent living, looking after myself again after having been so well looked after by others. My care team calls would begin again tomorrow with a morning call and a shopping trip with Lennon. I couldn't wait to tell everyone about my week's holiday and how well everything had gone – no 'what ifs'!

When I got home I unpacked all my washing into piles, ready to take over the laundry room in the morning. When I looked around my apartment at St Cuthbert's Court it did feel as if a week had passed. Everything had gone so smoothly and so well that I wondered if I had dreamed it all. I had a light supper, as I had eaten on the plane, then an early night, as I was planning to be up early, and I was tired after my long day. As I went to bed I thought to myself that I had succeeded in proving everybody wrong. I had got control of my life back.

On the Thursday morning I took over the laundry room as planned and did my washing. I would get my carer to hang the clothes up in my wardrobe later. With only two washing machines and two tumble dryers for 40 flats, they were always in use, so it was great place to meet people. The first person to hear about my holiday was Lennon, who was taking me shopping at 11.30 as well as doing the morning care call.

I found I could now put my damaged left arm on the handle of the shopping trolley while pushing with my right hand. This was a much more natural position, and I felt I was no different from any of the other shoppers. Lennon seemed quite taken aback by the new me and the fact that I could extend my left arm and rest it on the trolley. It was a big improvement in only a week.

That evening I was on the phone to Lexi for some time. She said she would pop in and see me on Saturday evening so we could have some time together.

On the Friday, Tablet Woman came as usual with my batch of medication. She was looking as gorgeous as ever, and she told me how well I looked, as did my friends Joanie and Den in the café across the road. That day I made a small but important change in my apartment, moving my small dining table slightly so that when I sat there I could look out of the big window into the garden and see and hear the birds, pigeons and sometimes seagulls. With the window open I would be able to hear them all. The seagulls came into land when it was cooler on the coast. Watching and listening to the birds singing their little hearts out in May was not something I had thought of before, but my holiday had changed everything.

That first Saturday home after my holiday was going to be a good one. The day started off with the little birds chirping away, the pigeons cooing and the seagulls laughing – it hadn't occurred to me before that seagulls laugh, but they do. I couldn't believe that I had not noticed any of this before. I decided that after a cooked breakfast with Joanie and Den I would go into town to get my holiday photos printed off from the memory card in my camera. I also made sure to pop into Thomas Cook and thank Lisa for making all the arrangements for my holiday at such a wonderful hotel.

My photos were superb, especially the ones of Michela and me. We all relive our holidays by looking at the photos afterwards. I stayed in town to have a glass of red wine at the mezze bar I liked. It felt great having the freedom to do this without needing anyone's permission or help. I was once again in control of my life!

It was so nice to see Lexi again, but she didn't like the pictures of me with Michela. Not much was said, but we did arrange to meet up the following Thursday for our usual Greek lesson. She no longer needed to meet me to help me down the stairs, so we met inside.

The following week my care visits started up again with my physio, social worker, clinical psychologist and the head of the stroke team, but it felt different this time as the meetings were held in my home and I was leading them.

Towards the end of May I decided to make a trip back to my home city of Nottingham, the place I should never have left. I would get to see my brother Darren and his wife Donna plus Molly and Jack, my niece and nephew, who I had not seen since my stroke. I wouldn't be able to see my dad of course. Not being able to go to his funeral still felt painful and haunted me, but now was my chance to at least visit his grave. Best of all I was going to TELL everyone I was going, not ask if I could! If I could travel 2000 miles to Cyprus, a couple of hundred miles would be a doddle. I would travel by National Express coach, which did a direct service from Newcastle to Nottingham with a break in Leeds. I would stay at the Ibis Hotel in the lace market in the centre of Nottingham, making it easy for me to meet up with friends in the evening. When I sat down I could now put my left hand on my left knee, a much more natural position, so I would show no visible signs that something was wrong, just a slight hobble and a limp when walking. I had the travel bug again! I bought myself a new small trolley case for this journey, the size they now class as a cabin bag, a perfect size for a three-night trip away. It would also be easier to handle on the walk from the bus station to Nottingham railway station. The Ibis Hotel was right by a tram stop, making it an ideal location. I planned to tell Lexi about my trip on the Tuesday when I was due to see her and the others at the Greek class. I wanted to make sure I didn't miss any classes now that our lessons would soon be coming to a sad end.

Lexi was still annoyed at me after seeing me so happy with another girl. I tried to explain, but she was having none of it and was just getting angrier. She asked why I had started a relationship with another girl when we were together, but Lexi and I were not together – I saw her once a week and wasn't allowed to phone her at home because she was still with her partner. So much for our running off into the sunset together!

My trip to Nottingham went very well, including the five-hour coach journey. Getting on and off the coach was easy, including getting off in Leeds to stretch my legs, after the practice I had had on my holiday, The steps up into the coaches were steep, especially if you were carrying hand luggage, but my small cabin case went in the hold. I chose a seat on the right so I could stretch out my left leg into the aisle as I had on the aircraft.

It felt good to be back in my home city, to meet up with my many friends there and to visit my father's grave. I also had time with my good friend Emilo, who owned an excellent Greek restaurant. I went to see him there and of course stayed for a meal and some red wine.

Back in Newcastle I was greeted with comments such as 'The wanderer returns!' from the managers at St Cuthbert's, Wendy and Margaret. They were becoming good friends, and they too could see a big difference in me since my holiday. Not only did I feel stronger and better in myself,

I'm sure my Greek had improved, thanks to Michela. I would find out when I went back to my Greek class.

I was still shocked at Lexi's reaction to seeing those photos, and from that moment we started to less of each other. It's true that I was thinking of Michela and remembering how she had made me feel whenever I saw her. I was also wondering how she would respond if I wrote to her to tell her about my feelings. The only way I could solve all this was to go back to Cyprus, something I was seriously starting to consider, as I was missing everyone and everything about the Constantinos the Great Hotel. I had never for a moment felt alone during my week there. I was also missing the heat of the sun on my body, specially now that the weather in the north of England had gone back to normal, chilly with thick grey skies and rain. My body had started to stiffen up again. Having once experienced that wonderful feeling of flexibility and freedom in my body, I wanted it again. I had been spending very little of my money, and what better to spend it on than something made me feel so good and so happy, and more importantly was so good for me? So I decided to go back to Thomas Cook and see Lisa, in the hope that a flight and a room at the Contantinos would be available in June. If I could, I was going!

It was good to see Lisa again. I simply said I wanted to go back, that month. Great news – the week of June 14 was available, a Wednesday flight again, just a month after I had left. I paid up, and that was that – job done. I had to stay in the agency for a while as it was raining heavily outside, so I accepted Lisa's offer of a coffee while she sorted out the holiday and printed all my details.

I now knew the procedure when it came to organising my medical cover. This time I didn't need to do a holiday clothes shop – I had everything I needed. I would take with me some boxes of chocolates for Michela, Sheri in the shop and Viktoria, to thank them for their help. I would get myself down to the big Boots store at Kingston Park for a sun lotion, a trip which would start the countdown to the new holiday. I knew I would be arriving at the hotel at about 3.15, just after Michela started her shift. Perfect timing!

Chapter 6

Cyprus again. And again...

For the journey to Cyprus I decided to keep to the routine that had worked so well for me before, starting with a taxi picking me up at 4 am. Remarkably, the girls on the Thomas Cook check-in desk remembered me, as did Gemma, a cabin crew member on board the aircraft, who looked after me very attentively without drawing the other passengers' attention to me. She was very beautiful and smelt good too as she leaned over to me to attend to the other passengers in my row. Again I had the aisle seat on the right so that I could stretch out my left leg. I was enjoying myself already!

It was too early for wine, so I settled for a coffee, and Gemma helped me with those little plastic pots of milk that are so frustrating to open with one hand. In the arrivals hall I looked for Anton, but this time I was on a Thomas Cook holiday so I would have one of their reps to meet me instead. I would still see Anton over the week. I felt more excited than I had the previous time, probably because I knew what I was expecting!

When I got to the hotel it seemed as if Michela was waiting for me. 'Hello!' she said sweetly, flashing me that wonderful smile. When she looked at me with those gorgeous hazel brown eyes I felt I was melting as I stood transfixed. It was Michela who checked me in, and there was a mischievous sexy glint in her eyes as she told me she had known I was coming because she had seen my name on the arrivals list.

Elias, the day porter, once again took my case as we went up to room 257, the one next to no 259, the room I had had on my previous stay. I couldn't wait to unpack, and soon I was back down in reception to give Michela her box of Thornton's chocolates. I knew she was going to like them, because Sheri had told me how much she liked chocolates.

I don't know how anyone can make 'thank you' sound as sexy as Michela did as our eyes met over the box. What I felt between us I couldn't explain, as I had never experienced anything this before. It felt so special, so wonderful, so priceless.

It was good to see the lobby bar again, and my first red wine time went very well – Paniyotis remembered me. 'You were here last month' he said. All the staff in the restaurant remembered me as well, and so did those in the shop. I gave Sheri a small box of chocolates to thank her for telling me what chocolates Michela liked.

As the weekend went on I enjoyed the social side of life in the hotel far more than I had the previous time, meeting and chatting to many more guests in the lobby bar after dinner. The hotel was far busier now than it had been in May. I got speaking two girls called Danielle and Niki, who were on holiday with their father. They were great fun and good company. I jokingly offered to take Danielle off her dad's hands and take her home with me, but he warned me that she was high maintenance! She was gorgeous and 'top totty', as was her sister, and they both talked like characters from East Enders. The effects of my stroke didn't seem to bother them – they saw beyond it and understood the person I was.

We were having such fun that I lost track of time, and soon it was midnight and Paniyotis was closing the bar. I could have carried on, but I knew I had had enough wine for one evening, so I said goodbye to the girls with hugs and kisses. I felt so good that I think I floated back to my room. When Danielle and Niki surfaced the next afternoon, they told me they had gone out to visit the busy bars of Protaras. I spent some time with them in the afternoon, and they looked great in their polka dot bikinis. It wasn't long before I started to feel very good again, my body so loose and flexible. How good would I feel if I came on a two-week holiday!

After speaking to my friend Erik the Dutchman, I decided that the next step for me was to get out of my comfort zone by leaving the hotel at night and go into the busy bars of Protaras, mixing with all the other holidaymakers. Erik agreed that on his next night off we would go out for a drink along the area that everybody called 'the Strip', the main road where all the shops and bars were located. So on his next night off we went to a bar called the Flora, about a 15-20 minute walk from the hotel. I felt so much more at ease now that I had my confidence back and there were far fewer visible signs that anything was wrong with me. The strip was packed with holidaymakers, but I don't think anyone noticed my limp as I went up to the bar and back.

Erik was amused that I wanted to get back to the hotel by 11 pm so that I could see Michela before she finished work. I wanted her to see that I could go out independently. My slight limp did not prevent me from keeping up with Erik as we made our way back to the Constantinos, weaving our way around the other holidaymakers, couples and friends out for the evening.

Back in the hotel, I was met by Michela's smile and those gorgeous hazel eyes. I felt a great sense of belonging back in the hotel, surrounded by so many good friends, a very different world from the solitary life I led in Newcastle. I didn't consider the people I shared St Cuthbert's Court my friends. They made no attempt to work but lived on benefits, and many were exploiting the system as well as they could – some of them had probably never worked.

I was now having long conversations in Greek with Mr Stathis, the hotel manager, which was helping to build my language skills. He often joined me at my table during dinner and ate with me. He also helped me to put together sentences I could use when talking to Michela, so I was now able to tell her how beautiful she was and how much I liked her eyes and her hair. Sometimes she would come to work with her hair up, and I told her I preferred it down, or *'protimo malia kato su'*. This all became part of our daily conversations, and she would still be a hard taskmaster if I got anything slightly wrong, explaining where I had gone wrong and making me say it again. I do think she was impressed by my efforts to speak good Greek.

Now that I felt so good, as if I had a new body, I wanted to find out what it could do, almost like getting a new car. I spoke to Anton, who suggested going on a day trip. There would be a holiday rep and I would be well looked after. We talked about where I should go and he suggested a trip to the capital, Nicosia. He warned me that this would be a full day out and a long coach ride, with a lot of walking. It would also be very hot, so it would be a challenge.

I booked the day trip with Anton, even though I wasn't a First Choice guest. We did a deal, and Anton agreed to go through the itinerary. He did not have many guests in the hotel and I knew he got commission on any trips, as did all the reps, which was why they always seemed to push them at meetings. So he would be helping me by looking after me, and I would be helping him. He would reserve a seat for me on the right, so I could stretch out my leg as before. I told Michela of my plans. She smiled and told me to be careful, but to enjoy my day out. 'I will miss you this day' she said. Her words sounded sincere and full of care.

Anton was right – it was going to be a long day, with an early pick-up at 7 am, and the coach would be nearly full. Nicosia was over 80km away. We would stay in a group, having some free time in the city, where we could take lunch and go shopping. I did have a nagging worry that as part of a group I might be letting people down with reduced walking ability – I didn't want to delay things or spoil anyone's day. Michela had organised a packed lunch for me from the restaurant, containing a couple of cobs (sandwiches), some fruit, a cold drink and a piece of cake. It was really sweet of her to do that.

Getting on and off these coaches was easy now, even with my backpack containing my packed lunch, a bottle of water, a book, sun cream, and of course my lunchtime medication. I don't think anybody on the trip that day even noticed me, and I mean that in the nicest possible way. I kept up with group as we were led – or marched! – around the old town and new town areas of Nicosia and my pace was similar to everyone else's. That made me feel very proud and pleased with myself.

In the old town I noticed a nice traditional taverna on one of the cobbled streets. There were bird cages around it, their occupants all happily chirping away. I had been nibbling on the packed lunch I had been given since we were picked up, so I decided to go back to the taverna for lunch. The old town was lovely, with many cobbled streets all lined with shops and eating places. Our stopping point was a big old church to which all the streets seemed to lead, so we thought it would be easy to find when we met back at the coach for the return journey.

It was very hot that day and I only needed a Greek salad with some 'Tiropita' cheese for lunch and a cold drink. The new town didn't interest me too much as it had all the big name stores I recognised from home, even a Debenhams right on the border point they call Checkpoint Charlie. Nicosia was also on the border of the occupied territory, otherwise known as Northern Cyprus since the invasion of Turkey in 1974; it is still occupied today. Only Turkey recognises this area, and on the map of Europe it is shaded grey.

When I got back to the hotel in the late afternoon, Michela was waiting for me at the entrance to see how I was and how my day had gone. It was the perfect opportunity for another photo together, and I had a picture taken with my arm around her. Her slender waist felt so good and it was a priceless feeling. It seemed to confirm that the 'relationship' we were building was more than just that between a receptionist and a guest. She seemed to see something she liked in me and to be able to see the person behind the stroke. It all meant a very enjoyable red wine time after a very good day, and I felt a great sense of achievement. Mr Stathis joined me again for dinner, and told me I was right to feel proud of myself. In the bar I told Anton all about my day.

I spent the rest of the holiday relaxing on my lounger in the sun, but it wasn't long before the week was coming to an end and once again I had to start saying my goodbyes. Again I started with Michela on the Monday evening, as the Tuesday was her day off. It felt different this time because we agreed to keep in touch with each other, swapping email addresses. Saying goodbye was the hardest part of the holiday. I went to see Sheri in the shop and chose a card so that I could write to Michela and tell her how I felt about her. I planned to leave it with Sheri to give to her, along with a cute teddy I had bought and a big bar of chocolate. Sheri kindly wrapped the teddy up with the card. I knew by now that she liked little furry animals.

I would now try to enjoy my last full day. It seemed to take longer going round this time, as I had made more friends during the week among the wonderful staff. Nothing was more heartbreaking than saying goodbye to Michela on the Monday evening and giving her a last hug and staring for the last time into those gorgeous eyes.

On the Wednesday morning I sat on the balcony

of my room looking at the wonderful views of the blue Mediterranean and drinking coffee to the sound of the little birds singing. My coach picked me up for the airport at 11 as before, and the journey home all went smoothly. I knew that by the time I got to Newcastle Michela would have arrived at work, opened my gift and read the card. I wondered what she would make of it. Perhaps she would be expecting it. I felt sure she would let me know in an email at the start of our first correspondence.

I woke up on the Thursday morning and checked my phone to find I had received a lovely email from Michela. If only I could have jumped on a plane and flown straight back to her!

My Greek lessons at the restaurant had finished, but I had now developed the confidence to go to the restaurant anyway and have a drink at the bar and a meal. I didn't feel as if I was on my own as I knew the owners so well. Being able to have my own 'red wine time' here made me feel part of society again. As a bonus I was going to give my Greek an airing on each visit, ordering my meal and wine in Greek. I would have liked Lexi to join me, but she wasn't happy that I'd gone back to Cyprus – she didn't see it as me going on holiday to do myself good, just as going back to see Michaela. Yet it was fine for her to go on holiday with her partner – talk about double standards! I began to see less of her from this point on.

During my red wine time at the bar in Simply Greek

that Tuesday, I suddenly had an amazing idea. After reading Michela's email again, it occurred to me that now she knew how I felt about her, the obvious thing to do was to go back and see her again. So on the Wednesday morning, only a week after getting home, I decided to go into town to see Lisa at Thomas Cook again and book another holiday that August. This time I would be able to email Michela and let her know I was coming back!

Good things were also happening at St Cuthbert's Court with the arrival of two new people, a nice retired couple called Eric and Christine. They seemed very genuine and more my sort of people than the other residents. David, who lived below me in the ground floor opposite, had now started to put food out for all the birds on one of two new bird-tables in the garden, putting out breadcrumbs, bits of bread and left-over pizza. They would all come swooping down and grabbing bits of food before taking off again, and I could sit and watch them from my window as I had my breakfast coffee. Unfortunately it wasn't usually the perfect blue sky I had got used to in Cyprus!

I was now having very few visits from my team of carers, so it came as a surprise when I had a call from Sheila, the physiotherapist, Helen, my social worker and Sharon, my OT, to say that they were all coming to see me to find out how I was doing, as they hadn't heard from me and had some important information for me. They all agreed how well I looked and how well I was doing. I told them it was all because I had been spending time relaxing in the sun and soaking up the vitamin D. It turned out I had been selected for a new trial and research project, which was starting straight away. It was called RATULS, which stood for Robot Assisted Training for the Upper Limb. The idea was to see how a robot linked to a computer could help people following a stroke by helping to train them to use their arms again. My sessions were held at North Tyneside General Hospital for 12 weekly sessions of one hour each. It was voluntary, but I would be expected to turn up for each session with a taxi to provide transport, a journey of 30-45 minutes.

I signed up to indicate my 100% commitment, but explained that my next holiday in August had already been booked and they would have to honour it. There were raised eyebrows and rolled eyes when they heard I was going on holiday again.

My sessions would take place every weekday at 10 am. I thought I would enjoy going to the NTGH, a nice new hospital near the coast at Tynemouth with views of the sea, even though of course it was the North Sea and not the Med. My first trip was to meet the RATULS team and have a full check-up to make sure I was fit enough for the trial. With no visits to RVI and now and not having seen a doctor for some time, I was apprehensive but interested in the outcome of the examination. I passed with flying colours, but more than that, I was told that all my nerve endings had come back on my left side and were at the same level as my right! All the other tests from my full 'MoT' were as they should be. This was brilliant news.

I signed up for the trial – it needed more signatures than opening a bank account – and met the team I would be working with. Each patient would be assigned a nurse/physiotherapist, and mine was called Leanne. She was a tall, this, sexy blonde with studs down the front of her overall which fastened in sexy sort of way, leading my imagination to run wild wondering what she was wearing under it! I was going to enjoy working with her. I also met Judith, who was going to be in charge of the trial. My news about the holiday was met with much side-nodding from Judith – me, a stroke victim, going on holiday! Leanne saved the day by saying she thought it was a good thing and brave of me to do it. It seemed I was a hero in her eyes (she had lovely blue eyes). Judith was worried about the time I would lose in the trial by being away for a week. Leanne stepped in again, saying she would formulate a new timetable for me to make up for the time I would miss by being on holiday, which only amounted to six sessions. Leanne suggested that I could do an extra 15 minutes each day until I had made up the time, and assured Judith it would work. I don't think Judith was too happy about this, but she didn't have much choice.

Despite my test results, there was a blow when it came to deciding which category I was going to be placed in for the trial, based on the amount of arm movement I had. I was in the bottom category – 'dead', the very worst. Dead meant exactly what it said. I doubted if I would ever see my left arm move naturally again; the damage to part of my brain had been too severe after lying on the floor for two and a half days.

Considering I was in the bottom category, the results from the sessions were very good. Each day the computer linked to the robot would produce a set of results which were kept until the end for the whole trial to be assessed.

It wasn't long before I was packing again for my third trip to Cyprus. This time Michela knew I was coming back as we had maintained contact with each other. Her emails had become quite mischievous as my visit approached, and she was challenging me to a tanning competition – we both knew there would be only one winner there as she was stuck in reception all day! I enjoyed the naughtiness of it all and it was great fun, and it made her happy, which made me happy! I decided to take her another teddy, the sort known as a 'tatty teddy' a cut little grey bear with a blue nose, plus another box of Thornton's chocolates. I had also got Sheri another small box of chocolates for all her help.

Once again my taxi was booked for 4 am, and this time it was a horrible wet morning. Once again Gemma was on the cabin crew. She remembered me and once again looked after me very intimately and attentively without drawing the attention of the other passengers. I now had a nickname my very own cabin crew member – 'Tinkerbell'.

When we got to the hotel, Michela was waiting for me at the entrance, which was really sweet of her, as was the welcome hug I received. I was in room 117 this time on the first floor, but still with wonderful views of the Mediterranean. It wasn't long before I had unpacked and gone down to reception to give Michela her new box of chocolates and her teddy and claim my prize for winning the tanning competition! Not that there really was a prize of course, or indeed a competition.

I was now ready for my first red wine time in the lobby bar with Paniyotis. Everyone I had met previously seemed to be there, except for my Dutch friend Erik, who had left to work in a hotel in the busy resort of Ayia Napa. Paniyotis said he would contact him to tell him I was back so that we could meet up.

I didn't need so much help in the restaurant now. With my balance stronger and my walking much better, I was fetching and carrying back my own meals. Only sometimes did I need help in cutting up meat, depending on what was on the menu. I found beef the most difficult. Viktoria was always on hand to help with this, and I got the impression she enjoyed doing it. I did try to pick meals that were easy to handle, as I did at home. My favourite was the stifado, a traditional beef stew, which was always on offer on Monday evenings, when it was 'Greek night'. Most nights there was a theme in the restaurant, so everyone's tastes were covered. I always got the same table each night, with Miranda making sure my table was reserved and ready for me at 7, after my red wine session in the bar.

Michela liked her cuddly toy, and of course the chocolates. You wouldn't think she ate chocolate to look at her, so slim and sexy. The look in her gorgeous hazel eyes when I gave her the gifts would render any man helpless. I always felt helpless and rooted to the spot when I gazed into them. 'There's no need for you to bring me something each time you visit, I'm just happy to see you' she said, but I wanted to and I could tell she liked them. I don't know what she was doing to me as I had never experienced it before – all I knew was how good I felt around her.

With the hot August sun warming my bones, it wasn't long before I was feeling great and moving freely and fluently around the hotel. I wanted to challenge myself again, so I spoke to my friend Anton and booked another day trip, as I wanted to see more of Cyprus, and after the success of my last day trip I felt ready for anything. I booked a day trip to Paphos on the west coast of the island, a big and busy port and resort with an airport. It would be another long day out, but Anton sold the trip very well and it sounded great. I told Michela in Greek what I was going to be doing. She was still a tough language teacher, but this was doing me good and my Greek was improving all the time.

When I told her about the trip, something happened that took me completely by surprise. Suddenly she said, 'You're not going. I don't want you to go – please don't go!' She blurted out these sentences in quick succession, then explained further. 'There is going to be a heatwave over the coming days with extremely high temperatures reaching 100 degrees Fahrenheit and high humidity,' she said. 'I would rather you stayed here in your office. If you stay here I will know you're safe and I won't have to worry about you.' My 'office' was the word she and the staff used for my lounger – Mr Stathis would ask 'what time is your office open?' meaning what time would I be getting to my lounger.

I was stunned into silence by all this. I didn't know what was happening. I had never experienced this before, even at the ripe old age of 49. Every word from those sweet, gentle lips sounded so sincere, genuine and caring. Once again this was proving to me that there was more to this friendship than a normal relationship between a receptionist and a hotel guest.

After she had said this, I went to see Anton and asked what would happen if I didn't go on the trip, and he said that because of my condition I could get my money back. He then asked me, with a knowing smirk, why I wanted to cancel. He had seen my intimate conversation with Michela, but he was surprised when I told him what she had said. I told him I had medical screening insurance and he said that would cover me. We would simply say I had not been well enough to go. I told Michela what Anton had suggested and she replied, 'It is good you stay here' and then added 'as you get to see me!'

I spent the rest of that day in my 'office' on the lounger, trying to take in everything that had happened and wondering if I really should drop out of the trip. If only I could be here in Cyprus and spend more time with Michela, maybe woo her and start to date her. Being around her was better than any medication or rehabilitation.

It was a good red wine time that evening. I didn't know what I was feeling, but I liked it! I exchanged a lot of good banter with Paniyotis as I told him of the day's events. From my stool at the bar I could see Michela in reception, and she was giving me lovely warm smiles all evening, keeping an eye on me all the time. I needed some advice, so I went to see Sheri. 'I can see you moving out here,' she said after I had told her of the events of the day.

Over the next few days I mulled over what to do about the day trip. After thinking about the risks involved, I decided that was Michela was right, and decided not to go, but I would follow Anton's plan in order to get my money back.

My pick-up was at 6.45 am, well before breakfast and my medication time. I had pre-arranged what to do with Anton. Once the driver of the coach found that I wasn't at the pick-up point he would ring the hotel and ask for my room number. I would be in my room to take the call and tell him I wasn't well enough to travel, making out that my walking would not be up to the day ahead. The driver would log all this and inform the company. It's strange how things can play on your mind, because when I got up that morning I did indeed feel ropey and quite light-headed.

It went as planned. The driver rang my room, I explained that I wasn't feeling well, and he said he understood and told me to inform my rep, who was of course Anton. The driver said he would make a note of our conversation and that I should tell reception, so I stopped at reception on my way to breakfast and explained my situation to them.

Now I would wait to see Michela again that afternoon to confirm to her that I hadn't gone on the trip. I will always remember the look of delight on her face and what she said. 'Paphos will always be there,' she told me.

My week in the sun was once again coming to an end and I was having to say my goodbyes again to all the wonderful friends I had made at the hotel. How could seven days pass so quickly? Indeed, how could a summer pass so quickly?

'Sorry is the hardest word' says the Elton John song, but it isn't – 'goodbye' is the hardest word to say. As always my first goodbye, and the hardest, was to Michela, on the Monday evening before she finished work. It took most of my last full day to go around my friends saying goodbye. Now that it was August I wasn't sure if I would be able to get back again that year, but Mr Stathis told me October was a good month to come to Cyprus as it still enjoyed fine weather but without the intense heat of the summer sun. We discussed this when he joined me for dinner at my table. Paniyotis in the bar had also told me that October was nice, and less busy.

I now knew my way around Larnaca Airport pretty well by now. After clearing security I headed for the atrium bar and passed the time to my flight relaxing with a soft drink and a bite to eat. When we boarded the flight, I recognised one of the passengers – it was Kayleigh, the attractive blonde nurse who had looked after me so well in the Cherryburn Unit, travelling home with her boyfriend. She seemed surprised to see me on a plane, coming back from holiday without a care worker. The last time she had seen me had been seven months ago in the unit, when I was still in a wheelchair. I had come a long way in that time, so it must have been a shock to her. I surprised her even more when I told her it was my third holiday of 2014.

I moved to an empty seat next to her so that we could talk. She said she hadn't had the best of holidays, and I told her how good the Constantinos the Great was. I asked how things were at the Cherryburn and she said nothing had changed – the nurses were still short-staffed and overworked and were having to do long hours for low pay, a common problem right across the NHS. Some of the patients who had been there while I was there were still in the unit – thank goodness I wasn't one of them.

Chapter 7

'I can see you moving out here...'

As before, when I got home my week in Cyprus seemed like a dream. I had agreed to return to my RATULS trial the following Monday morning to continue my work with the robot and get to see Leanne again at North Tyneside General Hospital. I had a few days to look forward to, with Tablet Woman's visit on Friday, and then getting my holiday photos printed off on the Saturday – specially those of me and Michela! I was getting used to doing this now, as were the staff of Robertsons, the local photo shop.

As always after returning from my week in the hot

sun, I felt so much better, stronger and more confident in myself, which may go some way to explain what happened next. First, out of nowhere on Friday afternoon, I got it into my head to ask Tablet Woman out to dinner! I have no idea where that came from – I just felt so very good, and I was buzzing with confidence. It wasn't a date, just dinner to say thank you and a chance to tell her how I felt about her. You see, Tablet Woman was the first in a long line of people since my stroke who had made me realise what a wonderful world we live in. Her visits gave me something to look forward to every Friday morning. In fact Tablet Woman, or rather Ashleigh, is one of the people I am dedicating this book to, people without whose help I might not be here. She had always come into my apartment to hand me my medication, so she must have felt safe around me. When she delivered medication to Eric at no 63, she would just push it through the letterbox.

It was easier to ask her out in the privacy of the flat, but unfortunately she said no. She said she was happy and living with someone. In truth I think she found it flattering to be asked out as it was not something that happened very often on her rounds.

I still couldn't understand why my home physio visits had been stopped due to NHS budget restrictions, while my visits from the social worker and clinical psychologist continued. I didn't need them now – I was in a good frame of mind. This might explain what happened next. During one of our chats, Helen, my social worker, asked me where I would like to spend Christmas. As it was still only late August, I thought it was a stupid question. I'm afraid I was now beginning to see these women as noisy old trouts poking their noses into my life. Only much later did I realise why you are assigned a social worker and a clinical psychologist after such a life-changing event. My answer was a bit tongue in cheek, in fact I went a bit too far when I said 'between Jennifer Aniston's thighs'. I soon got a letter from Newcastle City Council telling me I had made an inappropriate comment!

That was the last I saw of either of them, and I'm glad to say nothing came of the matter. It might not have been the right thing to say, but on the bonus side it did give me back control of my days, with no more visits from the ERD scheme. The only people who pressed my door buzzer now were Tablet Woman and the care team worker on her scheduled visits.

I was getting my life back in every way, and the next step in this was to bring an end to my ill-fated marriage to Gail. Yes, I was still officially married, not that it felt like it with everything that had happened. It would be a fairly straightforward divorce – I would just have to get the paperwork sorted – but it would still be costly. I knew I should never have got married or indeed left Nottingham. The meeting with my wife to discuss the divorce went smoothly. In a few months' time she would be my ex-wife.

She was going to find a solicitor and we would split the cost. Something else that was coming to an end was all hope of running off to a Greek island with Lexi.

Soon I was back at the hospital for more sessions in the robot trial. When I told Leanne, my nurse/physio, about my holidays, she told me how well I looked. She then said, 'Why don't you go for longer than a week?' To be honest this was not something I had thought about. I could of course go on holiday for as long as I wanted (funds permitting), as I wasn't working. I thought, if I felt so good after a week in the sun, how good would I feel after two weeks? This was something to think about for next year.

It was then that Leanne told me she was going on holiday in October, on a surprise trip booked by her boyfriend. She said she wouldn't know where she was going until she got to the airport. I asked about the trial and she said another nurse, Amy, would take over while she was away – unless I was away myself...

That got me thinking, and over the next few days I wondered if I could squeeze in one more week in Cyprus. It would set me up for the long English winter months. During my working years I had always made sure of taking a late summer holiday in October, believing it set me up for the long dark nights of winter. I remembered what Mr Stathis had told me about how nice Cyprus was in October. It would of course be so very good to see Michela once again. First I would have to get permission from Judith, the manager of the RATULS trial. I thought it might be another battle, but she was very fair – and I had my ace card to play, saying I would be away the same week as Leanne. Judith said the trial was due to finish at the end of October and reminded me of my commitment to it, but I had been a very good patient, with very good scores and favourable reports from Leanne.

First I had to make sure the flight and the hotel were available, which meant a trip to see Lisa again at Thomas Cook. She confirmed that they were, so I made the booking. Until then I had my trial to finish, and once again Leanne had worked out a programme to enable me to catch up after the missed sessions by doing a few more days into November.

Back at St Cuthbert's Court I was now beginning to get to know Eric and Christine very well. The three of us started going out for lunch over in Tynemouth on Sundays, using their car – I would offer to pay a share of the petrol. After lunch we would wander around the big market held every weekend on the platforms of the metro station; here you could buy anything. If it was a sunny day, Eric would drive us along the coast to St Mary's Lighthouse, where we would all get out of the car and take in the fresh sea air and great views, stopping for an ice cream van which was always parked in the same spot. This was certainly getting my life back!

My October holiday would be on the same 7 am Wednesday flight, and the business of boarding the aircraft had now become as easy and natural as it was for the other passengers. As I always checked in very early, I once again had an early sequence number, so I would be in the first group of passengers to board.

I would have liked to stop for a moment on the steps to look back and take in what I had achieved since leaving the stroke unit. If only all those doctors and specialists could see me now! Part of me is still convinced that everyone involved in my care would have been happier if I had given up after my stroke, as some of the other patients had done. It would have been easier to stick me in a wheelchair, stick me in front of the TV and turn me into one of the 'lifers' Kayleigh had told me about. That was never going to happen to me.

On board the aircraft I saw that Gemma was among the cabin crew and as usual she was very attentive to me, without drawing the attention of the other passengers. She said that when she knew I was on board she always offered to bring the coffee trolley so that she could help me with the little pots of milk. I thought it was really sweet of her to do this. The fact that she was very attractive was a bonus, of course! Again I was careful not to make eye contact with her during her demonstration of the emergency procedure, as we would always smile at each other. I'm not sure just how much the passengers would remember of this demonstration if we suddenly found ourselves plummeting to the ground at 500 miles an hour!

For this week in Cyprus I decided not to go on any day trips but to use the week just to relax in the sun and soak up the vitamin D to set me up for the winter months ahead. It would also allow me to maximise my time with Michela. And once again she was waiting for me at the entrance. It had been well worth travelling 2000 miles to see her. This time I was in room 303 on the top floor, on the pool side of the hotel, the sunny side. My room was further from the beach, but I still had a wonderful view of the blue Mediterranean from my balcony.

A couple of things happened during that week. First, Sheri said to me once again 'I can see you moving out here'. Also Michela said to me that she thought I would make a good Cypriot. Did she actually want me to move out there? It gave me something to think about during the week while I was relaxing on my lounger. With my relationship with Lexi dwindling away and my divorce pending, I had no ties in the UK except for my brother. Could it be done? It could be – couldn't it? What about my medication? What about Michela – what would she think of the idea? But Sheri had planted a seed in my head, and who knew what was going to grow from it? I had more questions than answers.

Something else that happened was that I met up with my Dutch friend Erik one evening to stroll down the strip and take in the night life. It was not as hectic as it had been during the summer months. The walk to the bar felt easier and quicker, and my walking was more fluent than before. Again Erik made fun of me because I wanted to get back to the hotel before Michela finished at 11 pm.

When we got back there was a karaoke evening going on in the pool bar. I had done karaoke before my stroke many times, my signature song being 'What a Wonderful World' by Louis Armstrong, sung in an imitation of his voice. I wasn't sure if I would still be able to do this while having to think about my balance and stand still and upright for the duration of the song – would holding a microphone in my right hand affect my balance?

There was only one way to find out. With my Dutch friend beside me for support, I had a go with the last song of the evening. All went fine – I could still do karaoke! I think what pleased me most was that I didn't even think about the visual signs that there was something wrong with me as I stood in front of the audience, another sign that my confidence was back to full strength.

For some reason I didn't go back downstairs to the pool bar area for the last few days of my holiday. I told Michela about my singing and she said I should tell her next time as she wanted to hear me sing 'What a Wonderful World'. I told her I had chosen that song because it reminded me of her and I was going to come back next year anyway, in the same months, May, June August and October. Now I had to come back – to sing to Michela! Again she said she could see me coming out to Cyprus to live. She also mentioned that the hotel stayed open through the winter, although all the bars, restaurants and clubs closed from the end of October until the beginning of May. The only problem would be that the three main British tour companies didn't fly to Cyprus during the winter – there was only Mercury Direct, an on-line-only agent. So it looked as if I would have to wait until May, which would be a long time to wait to see her again. At least I would be able to go to the lessons at the Eldon Square Language Centre, which would give something to over the dark winter nights. I wanted to do well to improve my Greek and impress Michaela.

This time my round of goodbyes was harder than ever, knowing I would not be back for seven months. For my goodbye hug with Michela I wore some aftershave, Spice Bomb by Victor and Rolf, which was Lexi's favourite. Michela commented that I smelt nice, which meant a lot to me. She asked if I was on Facebook, because it was easier and quicker than email, and we agreed that I would create an account so that we could communicate better. I was all for this, as I knew my brother Darren was on it. I would make a trip to Nottingham, where he could set me up with an account, as I didn't have a clue how it worked. I told Michela I would find her on Facebook as soon as my account was set up.

I didn't bring her any chocolates or a soft toy out on this trip as I wanted to leave something for her as a surprise on her return to work on the Wednesday. On my last day I sought the help of my friend Sheri in the hotel shop and picked a card so I could again write to Michela telling her how she made me feel and how I felt about her. This time I picked a cuddly cat for her. Sheri gift-wrapped it and promised to give it to Michela the following day. I spent my last day as usual going around saying goodbye to everyone.

There was a sense of sadness as I unpacked my holiday clothes back home for the last time in 2014. I got a thank-you email from Michela, again saying she liked my card and gift very much but I didn't have to get her anything.

I wouldn't be long before I would be packing my cabin bag again as I decided to travel to Nottingham, partly to see how well I could cope with rail travel. I would take the National Express coach to Nottingham, but I would then take the train to Mansfield, only a 40-minute journey from there. I wanted a new Mansfield Town football shirt, and I could get one on a morning trip out. It would give me some exercise, as I would also have a good walk to the Field Mill football ground from Mansfield Station. October was an important month, as it would be a year on the 11th since my Dad died, and the trip would give me a chance to pay my respects again. This would also be a chance to see Darren and his family and have a night out with my many friends there – they would see huge change in me now that I had got my confidence back.

My trip to Nottingham was successful and very enjoyable. Darren and I agreed that I would spend Christmas with him and his family, staying in their spare room, which would be far better than spending it on my own in my flat. I would be the first time we had spent Christmas together since we were kids. Darren was the more settled and responsible of the two of us, because while he had got married, bought and house two kids I had been the nomad, searching for something but not knowing what – until now, perhaps.

Darren said that over Christmas he would show me how to set up a Facebook account, so I needed to buy an iPad or tablet. I knew Darren's kids, Molly and Jack, would enjoy having their Uncle David around at Christmas as they used to have my dad over on Christmas Day, and I was looking forward to seeing my niece and nephew and opening the presents on Christmas Day.

Getting into October was a reminder that a year before I had been in the Cherryburn Stroke Unit on a hoist, unable to stand or walk unaided. After the year I had had, all that now seemed a lifetime away.

Back at St Cuthbert's, I had an interesting conversation in the communal garden with Eric, who said he had been to see a chiropodist on Gosforth High Street. I agreed to go with him on his next visit and was introduced to the chiropodist, Shirley. I sat down with her to explain what had happened to me and why I needed a chiropodist or podiatrist. She was impressed that I knew that the word 'podiatrist' came from the Greek 'podia' for foot. My Greek skills had come a long way, and I was sure I would do well on the new language course. Shirley told me she could feel a good pulse in my left foot, just as strong as in my right, which meant my circulation was fine, so my brain and heart were working well together, something the 'what if' people had been worried about. Shirley also saw to my feet and cut my toenails, something which I struggled with.

My new Greek classes would begin at 7 pm like the previous ones, which was good news as it fitted in with my care plan. I decided that afterwards I would have a take-away roast lamb dinner with all the trimmings at the Luv Ur Grub café across the road from St Cuthbert's Court. This meant no preparation, washing up or tidying up afterwards. Lexi was going to attend the class – I'm not sure why, as we were no longer going to run off into the sunset together, and her partner seemed to have no interest in the language – or her! I had my own reason for wanting to go to classes and improve my Greek – Michela!

It felt strange seeing Lexi, as she had slowly and gently slipped out of my life, saying my attentions were elsewhere. I disagreed of course, but Lexi wouldn't have it, saying I was free to go on holiday, so why did it have to be Cyprus? Perhaps she was looking for an excuse to get out of this relationship following my stroke and the condition it had left me in, with the visible signs that something was wrong with me. I was dealing with this, and my trips to Cyprus were helping. Michela on the other hand saw the man behind the stroke and liked me for the person I was.

I believe this gave Lexi the perfect opportunity to get out of the relationship without causing me any unnecessary heartache. In truth our dream of running away to a Greek island had been smashed by the stroke. But maybe Lexi was right, and it was Michela I really wanted. I knew that I wouldn't have got to where I was in my life without her. She had shown me what a beautiful world we have around us, at a time when I wanted to hate the world and what it had done to me. We are all so wrapped up in our own little worlds that we don't appreciate the things around us, simple things like listening to the birds chirping away in the morning, something I took no notice of before my stroke. What a shame it took something so devastating to make me appreciate this.

The language course was expensive at £300, but it covered three courses each of 10 lessons. It would be intensive, giving me focus and something to do over the winter months. This course was run by a professional language teacher, Andrini, who was from the island of Kefalonia.

We were a group of six including me and Lexi, and I didn't see her until she walked into the room. The first thing we all learned was how to introduce ourselves, how to say our names and ask for each other's names, which was clever as it broke the ice in the group. I could feel the difference already with a professional teacher. Andrini had a fair but no-nonsense approach. Everything we learned in class was printed on paper, and he advised us to create our own folders, adding to the folder as each week went by – and we got homework! Each of us was given a task which we had to read out to the class the following week. I was doing very well in the lessons. I wouldn't say I was the best in the class, but I thought I was in the top one! This was much to the annoyance of Lexi and the others in the group, and they gave me the label of teacher's pet!

Because I was doing well, I formed a good rapport with Andrini, who often picked me to read my homework to the class. With the RATULS trial now complete, I would miss my daily trips to the NTGH and Leanne. Looking back on the trial, I feel it was a privilege to have been one of the 600 people to have taken part. My scores would perhaps help other stroke victims in the future. I now had more time to fill as I please, allowing me to get out more and get back into society.

Michela was still keeping me up to date with events at the Constantinos the Great hotel. I missed her and all my friends back in Cyprus, but we would have more contact once I had joined Facebook at Christmas. I would get Lennon to help me choose a tablet device as he knew about these things – I didn't!

November 2014 would bring another anniversary and a day of reflection. The 8th was the first anniversary of my dad's funeral. It still hurts today that I wasn't allowed to go. Looking back gave me the chance to review my progress and consider how much better I was doing. It also brought the risk of thinking about those dark days and the things I could no longer do, like jump in the air, kneel on the floor or lie down on my front (as I wouldn't be able to get up again).

I had now become more emotional as I learned to deal with all my emotions again, because of the neurological condition the stroke had left me with. I guess this is why you are assigned a social worker and a clinical psychologist after such a life-changing event, and I realised that it wasn't really fair to call them nosey old trouts. I was learning, and maybe mellowing a little. Should I be giving my fellow residents of St Cuthbert's Court a second chance, and not be so judgmental? If I could make some new friends it would stop the feelings of isolation I still had, and open up some new opportunities. But some of them had drink problems, and those who abused alcohol had no place in my life. But perhaps I was better off on my own after all, and Sheri's comments that she could see me moving to Cyprus were very appealing, along with Michela's sweet comment that I would make a good Cypriot. Could that happen? I was doing so very well, yet it was still the early days of my rehabilitation, and with no quick fix it was going to be a long road to recovery, but at least I was on that road. I had to remind myself that it was only ten months since I had been discharged from the stroke unit and only eight since I had been able to cast aside my wheelchair. In that short time I had flown eight times!

My December trip to Nottingham was booked in advance. I would be travelling down with National Express on December 22 and again staying two nights in the Ibis Hotel, meeting up with many friends for Christmas drinks, chat and laughter. I would travel to my brother's for lunch on Christmas Eve and stay with him until the 27th, when I would travel back to Newcastle. I wanted to enjoy this Christmas, having missed out last year because I was still in the Cherryburn Stroke Unit, and no matter how hard the nurses and staff tried to make it feel like Christmas, I was stuck in a hospital and hated it! And at the time I hadn't known what sort of future lay ahead of me, and all the good things that would happen.

Then, with my Christmas trip all arranged and paid for, Michela emailed me out of the blue to ask if I wanted to have Christmas at the hotel! Much as I wanted to see her and all my friends, and enjoy some winter sun, I didn't want to let Darren and his family down after so kindly inviting me to stay, and the kids would be looking forward to it. And as I mentioned above, although the Constantinos the Great hotel stays open through the winter, the rest of the resort closes down and you can't fly from Newcastle, so the logistics of it all would just be too difficult. I replied to Michela with a heavy heart to explain all this.

It wasn't long before I was packing for Nottingham. There didn't seem much point in putting up Christmas decorations with me going away, so I didn't bother. I was soon on the coach, which gave me a chance to look at my tablet device, which Lennon had chosen for me in Tesco on one of our shopping trips. I had told Michela to look out for my Facebook friend request on Boxing Day! This would be the first time I had spent Christmas with Darren since 1997 when I left the family home to go and live with my girlfriend at the time.

It felt so very good to be able to meet up with all my friends in Nottingham. We met up in the Christmas market set up in the centre in front of the Council House and drank glühwein and mulled wine from some of the many huts put up to create a German market, which all looked very Christmassy. The mulled wine had a lovely smell of cinnamon and oranges. Glühwein is spiced red wine, served and drunk hot – wonderful on a cold winter's night and its aroma always reminds me of Christmas. It is very popular in countries such as Germany, the Czech Republic and Poland.

After two 'glühwein nights' it was time to leave the Ibis, which was a shame as all the cheeky girls remembered me from my October visit and were very friendly. I even sat near them at the bar for my 'red wine time'.

Christmas with Darren and Donna was great. Donna cooked Christmas dinner for 12 people, including a large number from her family as well as me. It went over three sittings and was controlled like a military operation. My father had always spent Christmas Day at Darren's, and although he would say it was 'just another day', he always tried his best and did what he thought was right for his grandkids, even wearing a Santa hat which read 'Santa is a Forest fan'. He made sure he had plenty of photographs taken of him wearing it!

The previous Christmas had been quiet because Dad had only just left us, but this year I was more than happy to step in and play the daft uncle to make Molly and Jack laugh. They missed their 'Granddad Cricket', as they called him. I wasn't trying to replace my dad as I could never do that, but it was good to enjoy Christmas together. It is sad at Christmas when you miss those who have gone. What I would give for one last chat with him, to hear his deep voice just one more time. I wonder what he would make of what had happened to me. I would have asked his guidance about my plans for the future. I'm sure he would tell me to get on with it – it was my life now. It's not the fact that someone dies that hurts the most, it's the idea that you will never see them again or hear their voice that hurts, The Dalai Lama once wrote ' In grief time has no boundaries', which is so very true as we never forget those who have gone from us.

On a lighter note, it was fun to see Jack and Molly open their presents on Christmas morning. They were older now and didn't believe in Santa Claus any more – they knew how it worked and they knew about credit cards! But there was still something special about seeing all the wrapped presents around the Christmas tree, and there was still that thrill of ripping the paper off the presents and seeing what you'd been given – even for me!

Boxing Day brought more joy and excitement as I finally joined the Facebook revolution. Darren was the first friend request I sent, followed of course by Michela. We were also connected by Messenger and we could have live chat and make calls. Our communication would now be much quicker and easier. I also found some of my friends in Cyprus on Facebook, including Sheri.

The two days at my brother's passed all too quickly and I was soon travelling back to Newcastle to have a quiet New Year's Eve on my own in my apartment looking back on what a great year 2014 had been. 2015 promised to be even better! I wasn't sure how many times I would be going back to Cyprus, but it was the way forward, because I felt so wonderful when I was out there, so I would be going as often as I could. I now had some money I had inherited from my dad, and I'm sure he would have agreed for me to use it on going there as it made me feel so much stronger and fitter. I did treat myself to a big, comfortable reclining chair to relax in in my flat while watching the large-screen TV I had also bought.

I had a nice surprise on getting home – Leanne had sent me a Christmas card. I must admit that the thought of sending one to her hadn't crossed my mind. I had a quiet New Year's Day at home watching TV and sending Happy

New Year messages on Messenger, trying to remember that my friends in Cyprus were two hours ahead. I was beginning to feel that the stroke hadn't taken my life away – it had given me one. It had shown me a new life, a new way of doing things. I did however miss work – getting back to work would be an objective for the year ahead, and would be good to be earning again as I was now down to minimal sick pay and topping it up with benefit payments. But I had paid into the state for over 30 years, so I felt I was entitled to something back. I wasn't sure what sort of work I could do though, with no natural movement in my left arm and limited walking ability.

The alternative of course was to move to Cyprus to be near my new-found friends, living in a better climate with a much more relaxed lifestyle. It was just a question of what I would do for money. The new year certainly wasn't going to be a boring one. I had a lot to look forward to.

After the Christmas and New Year break my Greek class resumed, and I was delighted to be told by Andrani that I didn't need to take the third part of the course as I had come on so well during the first two. I could now read and write some Greek as well as speaking and understanding it. I practised by sending Michela a 'thinking of you' card I wrote, which she appreciated very much. I would miss my Tuesday nights out. I didn't want to gloat when I heard that Lexi had been told she would need to do course three!

Not that we spoke much now as we very jealous of my Cypriot receptionist.

It was disappointing to leave the Greek course without some kind of certificate, but I suppose my 'certificate' was that I could now communicate in Greek, at least a little. I had saved all my coursework in a binder. I decided that I would have a revision day on Tuesdays and spend the afternoon going through my binder. This would keep my Greek fresh and keep my brain active, important with the neurological damage I had suffered. I could of course still have my Tuesday lamb dinner at Luv Ur Grub across the road.

I was determined that 2015 was going to be a good year. I was feeling so good about myself. Yes, I had lost the use of my left arm, but I still had my speech, I could walk, and most importantly, my mind and my memory were intact.

I was officially still employed by John Lewis, but now that I was on the minimum sick pay I needed to earn some money. I asked for meetings with the management of the firm about this, which seemed to surprise everyone, as I had the option of not going back to work and claiming benefits to top up my sick pay, but this wasn't for me. Work was all I had known since I had left school in 1981 until 32 years later when I had my stroke. Unfortunately, for health and safety reasons and John Lewis's duty of care towards me, they told me I would be unable to return. There was also a concern about me getting to and from work safely – more 'what ifs'. With the claim culture that had developed, if something happened to me at work all sorts of companies would be circling around like vultures pressing me to make a claim against John Lewis, something I would not have done as they had been very good to me and as a firm they are well known for looking after their staff, or 'partners'. Everything in a store involves lifting and handling, so there wasn't a suitable job for me to do.

Discussion then turned to an ill health pension retirement deal, which would mean me getting a monthly pension payment and a small lump sum. This would be a very useful opportunity to carry out my plan to move to Cyprus.

As it turned out, in 2015 I would again visit Cyprus four times, devoting some of the time to research into the possibility of living there. If I was going to do it, I would need to plan it properly and not act on a whim. There was lots to sort out regarding medication, finding a place to live, what to take with regarding personal belongings and – and of course, how to get out there with all my stuff. I was going to do all the planning and decision-making myself, as I wanted to prove everybody wrong by showing I could still do all these things, along with problem solving. I was going to do this on my own, with a little help from my friends.

There had been no repercussions following the incident

with the social worker, but I did have to see a new one, as I would have to let everybody involved in the ERD scheme of my plans, which direction I chose to go in.

Chapter 8

A surprise for Michela

Before I could think about moving to Cyprus, I had to sort out all my remaining ties to the UK. The first thing was the divorce, and Gail came round to my flat so that we could fill them in together – she had more experience with this sort of thing as she had been divorced twice before. It would take perhaps a month or two before the divorce became legal.

I was enjoying my time on Facebook getting to see what my friends were up with their posts and updates. I learned that Michela's birthday was April 4, so I had the idea of making a surprise visit to Cyprus to see her then. That wouldn't work though, as she would see my name on the advance booking and then the arrivals list. I did send her a birthday card written in English and translated into Greek, knowing it would make her smile and she would appreciate the effort I was making. I sent the card a couple of weeks in advance, knowing it would take 10-14 days for it to get to Cyprus. I would have so liked to have been there for her birthday and some early sun, but it was still the winter season and flights were still infrequent. However it would only be another month until May, when the summer season would start.

I asked Michela if she was going to have a party and wear a sexy dress, and she replied that she was just going to have drinks with a few friends and that sexy clothes weren't her style, she would rather dress casually and for comfort. I would still have liked to see her in a sexy dress. I thought she was a photographer's dream, with those gorgeous hazel brown eyes and that smile of warmth and beauty.

Soon I was back at Lisa's desk in Thomas Cook in Newcastle. Everything was available and to my surprise they had the same 7 am Wednesday flight. I wondered if Gemma, my little Tinkerbell, would be among the cabin crew. Soon it was all booked. I knew things would be very different this year. I would be able to enjoy the build-up to my first trip much more as I was a different person now, much stronger physically and mentally. The only people I had to tell were Ashleigh, my Tablet Woman, so she could deliver two weeks' supply of medication before I went away, and the care team, who would cancel my calls for that week.

I was delighted to see that Gemma was indeed on the Larnaca run for the new summer season, and there she was on board the aircraft. She again remembered me, and it was lovely to see her. Although I was so much stronger now, I still needed help with the little milk pots. We had time for a chat as she came along serving coffee and drinks during the flight.

Once in Cyprus I started telling my closest Greek friends about my plans in the hope of getting some information about areas to live, starting with my friend Sheri in the hotel shop. 'I told you you'd end up moving here,' she said. 'Have you told Michela?'

Michela was next, and I waited for a quiet moment in reception before telling her. She said to me, 'It will be a better life for you here, but I don't want you to move to Cyprus because of me.' Like most of the staff of the hotel, she lived in the nearby city of Paralimni. Protaras, where the hotel was, seemed the ideal place to live, but it closed down in the winter, so Paralimni would be much better for me. She suggested looking at the area of Kapparis along the coast. It had many shops and pubs and there was a large ex-pat British community, as well as plenty of local Cypriots, so I could continue to practise my language skills. Sheri also lived in this area, and they both promised to start looking for a suitable place for me, a ground-floor one-bedroom apartment if possible. Now that we were all connected on Facebook, they could send me details of their findings.

'I believe a move to Cyprus will be good for you, a better life,' said Michela. I could tell that she had more to say to me. 'But I don't want a prince to come and save me on a flying horse. And you don't need to keep buying me gifts, but I do like it and I like the attention you give to me.'

It seemed she was fighting her emotions. Then she flashed me that beautiful smile, the one that made me feel like a prince. If only I could move to Cyprus – if only it could be that simple! If I was a prince, Michela could be my Andromeda, the beautiful princess from Greek mythology, and I could be her prince Perseus, who saved her on his winged horse Pegasus.

I had a chat with Mr Stathis, and he agreed that Kapparis would be a good place to live, only 15 minutes away and on the coast. I could feel a plan coming together. There was a new entertainment team in the hotel this year, two lads and two girls: Angus (who I renamed Rufus), Oliver, Chelsea (who quickly became my Angel of the North), and Kelly. Chelsea, who was from Sunderland, offered to rub sun cream on my right arm, the one place I couldn't reach of course. She had seen me struggling to do this as I sat on my lounger. She offered to help, and I was only too willing for her to do so! I quickly became well known to the four of them and we became good friends. I asked them if we could have a karaoke evening so I could sing for Michela, and they agreed. I told her I was going to sing 'What a Wonderful World' and she said she would listen and give a score out of 10. I gave my song everything, and it went well, with Chelsea helping me to get up on to the stage my Dutch friend Erik had built. The score she gave me was 12! I told her I would sing again when I returned in June.

So far I had never gone into the hotel pool, through a mixture of apprehension and wanting to take things slowly on my road to recover. But Mr Stathis said it was now time I tried it, with the help of two of the new team, Angus and Chelsea, who would come into the pool with me in their One Stop entertainment uniforms, orange T-shirts and shorts, with Mr Stathis watching in his white shirt and trousers like a manager taking a coaching session. I felt confident walking into the pool, holding on to the handrail as I went down into the water. Once I was in the pool I had fun bouncing up and down and singing the Tigger song – 'The wonderful thing about Tiggers is that Tiggers are wonderful things', which made Kelly laugh – she was watching alongside Mr Stathis. Chelsea's T-shirt soon became very wet! I felt a great sense of achievement, as well as having fun. Exercise in a pool like – hydrotherapy – is very good for a recovering body. Mr Stathis told me he had seen my progress over the five holidays and told me you couldn't compare the way I had been a year ago with the way I was now. Hearing my friend's warm words confirmed my feeling that I had changed the direction of my life.

I couldn't believe it when I realised I had spent a whole hour in the pool. No wonder I was getting tired, bouncing up and down and pretending to be Tigger! Feeling very pleased and proud of myself, I took great delight in going to tell Michela of my latest achievement. We would have hugged, but I was soaking wet and I didn't to get her uniform wet.

I spent the rest of the afternoon relaxing on my lounger, and Chelsea rubbed sun lotion into my right arm again. She certainly was my angel of the north. The new year seemed to be bringing me new hope.

As always, my week had gone too quickly and was soon almost over. Again on the Monday evening I had to say goodbye to Michala, and again I chose a cuddly toy and a card for her. Sheri went to a supermarket to get my lovely princess a box of Belgian chocolates.

Leaving was so difficult, yet somehow I once again enjoyed the flight home – maybe one reason was that I could have a small bottle of wine with Gemma, who would open it for me. Again she was so attentive and affectionate without drawing the attention of the other passengers.

As always after my week in the sun, I felt so much better and my walking was more fluent, but there was more this time. I felt I was taller and standing straighter as my body continued to repair itself. I thought how good I would feel if I had the sun every day. Another stone had been laid in the road to blue skies and red wine!

I had promised myself that I would go back in June as I had last year, and it wasn't long before I was visiting Lisa again to book it. However the Wednesday flight had become very popular, and I found I would not be able to get a flight and a room at the Constantinos the Great until early July. In fact this would prove to work out well as I had to attend more meetings with the John Lewis pension department to work out an ill-health pension package we could agree on.

Always looking to improve myself, I changed my revision plan for my Greek course, moving my revision day to Wednesday. On a Tuesday evening I would now take myself out to the Simply Greek restaurant for a meal and a few glasses of red wine, ordering in Greek and chatting with Dimitri and Anna, with some exchanges in Greek. Tuesday evening was quiet as the restaurant was quiet and I didn't have a care call that day.

I would still go shopping with a member of the care team to do my big weekly shop at Tesco, but now I pushed the trolley around myself, putting the items I wanted into it. All the carer did was drive me to the retail park and back, unload the trolley at the checkout and pack my goods. As June went on I started to do my little top-up shop at the small Asda branch in Wansbeck Road. That was too far to walk there and back, so I would get a taxi for the short ride. I felt strong enough to do my own shopping and carry the basket around with me. This made me feel good, as it was all part of my independent living. It was also good practice, because if I went ahead with the move to Cyprus I would be doing my own shopping. In fact I would be doing everything on my own, as I would be turning my back on all the help on offer in the UK – however accepting that help would mean not taking back full control of my life, as I wanted. This was why the move was gaining momentum. Everything now seemed to be moving in the right direction, the 'onwards and upwards' attitude!

I couldn't wait to get back to Cyprus, knowing it was going to be a big week for me rehabilitation wise as I would be in the pool most days. I also had my research to continue with. Before that, I had things to do. I needed to update my holiday wardrobe, with swimwear and clothes for the evening as well as shorts and T-shirts. I would take myself to Matalan, where I could get everything I needed. I was feeling more confident about going out for red wine time in the evening. I also needed to go into town to buy Michela some Thornton's chocolates, which were available in a small bag containing all the favourites, as well as another cuddly toy and a card. I also decided to get a bag of chocolates for Gemma.

As I waited at the airport for the gate number to come

up on the screens, I saw the Thomas Cook crew pulling their cases along. There was no sign of Gemma, but as I walked to the gate later I recognised her sexy, slender figure in front of me. I managed to catch up with her and gave her the chocolates. She seemed surprised but happy with my gesture, and we had a hug. I wanted the flight to Larnaca to last more than five hours, as Gemma was all smiles. Gemma did seem to like me, and it wasn't out of pity – I felt there was a genuine affection. Upon arrival at Larnaca, I suddenly realised that I was reading and understanding all the signs in Greek!

Reception was crowded when I got to the hotel and Michela was busy getting ready for the next coachload of guests to arrive – I could see the line of passports. I found I would be in room 117, the same one I had stayed in the previous August. I decided to leave my unpacking for now, as I wanted to get back down to reception to give Michela her card and gifts. She was still busy as the next coach had arrived and all the guests were jostling for attention. She knew I had something for her and cheekily made it difficult for me to give them to her. I did get a chance in the end but it was a short encounter, and I said I would see her later. Then I went to look for my friends Angus and Chelsea to find out when and where there was going to be a karaoke evening during my stay. They told me it was tonight! That meant I would be going straight into my performance of 'What a Wonderful World' for Michela – they had planned it. They also told me they had made plans for me to get into the pool each day – brilliant – I was all for that!

I passed by reception to tell Michela about the karaoke session, and again she told me I had didn't have to buy her things. I said 'But I want to,' and again she flashed me that smile of warmth and beauty and our eyes locked in a gaze as if there was an electrical field between us. I was rooted to the spot, transfixed. This had never happened to me with anyone before.

It was soon red wine time, which would be in three parts tonight. Part one was before dinner, sitting at the bar as always and chatting to Paniyotis. Mr Stathis joined me at the bar to have some 'time out' and we talked about my plans to move to Cyprus and how good it would be for me to spend most of my time out in the sun. I classed this chat as part of my research project – after all, I wanted as much information as I could get. He told me he would oversee my time in the pool again and wanted to see me in it every day, not just lazing around in my 'office'. 'Do this, and at the end of the week you won't need any help getting out of the pool,' he said. I agreed, telling him that was what I wanted to. 'On your next visit you go into the sea,' he said. He was talking like a football coach. How that would be something!

I no longer needed so much help with my dinner, and my balance was good enough for me to carry a full plate back to my table. Even so, Viktoria was always happy to assist me. Part 2 of red wine time was back at the bar after dinner, when more guests were present, but somehow I managed to claim my favourite stool at the bar. Soon after that I was downstairs in the pool bar for red wine time part 3, getting myself 'into the zone' for my performance.

Considering how busy the pool was, the audience at the bar was small. Chelsea helped me onto the stage, and my performance went well. I very much enjoyed it, particularly as I knew the song well now, and I also knew that Michela was in reception listening to me singing for her.

When the song had finished I saw Chelsea looking up at the terrace above the stage and turned round to see that Michela had come out onto the balcony to listen to me. That was breathtaking – a priceless moment! I felt so good that I stepped down off the stage without any help – I simply forgot I was supposed to need it. As I headed upstairs to see Michela and get her score for my performance, her smile of warmth and beauty seemed to pull me towards her. She told me my score this time was 12.5 out of 10! I almost skipped downstairs to tell Angus and Chelsea my score, then back up to say goodnight to Michela before she finished her shift. It had been a long but very good day. Tomorrow I would wake up to begin my holiday in the sun!

I woke up to a perfect blue sky and had coffee on my balcony listening to the little birds and looking over the Mediterranean, which again looked like a sheet of pure blue glass. I was still buzzing from last night's perfect moment seeing Michela on the balcony.

I had my usual breakfast of Greek yoghurt, banana, fruit and honey, washed down with orange juice and several coffees. Viktoria helped me as usual with opening the little tubs of honey. Then it was time for my medication – I had kept to the same routine for that ever since my days in the stroke unit.

I felt much more confident walking down into the swimming pool with Angus in front of me and Chelsea behind, while Mr Stathis watched from the sidelines. Once again, Kelly was amused as I bounced up and down in the pool singing 'The wonderful thing about Tiggers is that Tiggers are wonderful things'. If only I had done this last year! But like anything on the road to recovery, it was all about timing and taking everything one baby step at a time. There was no quick fix. I began to realise that there was a serious side to this, as I was doing something – jumping up and down - I could no longer do on dry land, thanks to the weightlessness the water gave me. That's why astronauts do a lot of training in water. Bouncing up and down was making me use my legs muscles in a different way, so it was no wonder I got tired and my legs ached.

Mr Stathis was right. As the week went on I could soon have got in and out of the pool on my own, but my friends enjoyed helping me. Mr Stathis told me to bring my camera so he could take some photos. He enjoyed watching me, and it got me out of the office – it made a change from the day-to-day running of the hotel.

My next mission, with the help of Angus and Chelsea, was to get into the sea.

During red wine time that Thursday evening, I asked Anton if there was a short day trip I could go on that wouldn't interfere with my pool time. Although I was on a Thomas Cook holiday I wanted to go with his company, First Choice, as he could get me a good deal and he would get commission for selling me the trip. He told me had a half-day trip to Famagusta, setting off early in the morning and back early afternoon. That was perfect, even more so as the trip was on a Saturday. I had to act quickly, as I felt like having some time out and my week would soon be over.

With a few glasses of red wine inside me, I had another crazy idea – I would ask Michela out on a date! I would take her to Famagusta with me. I believed that if we had some time together, something special might happen. She would not miss work, as she would be back in time for her shift at 3 pm. I told Anton of my plan and he thought it was a great idea and said she would be pleased to be asked out. All I had to do was to pluck up enough courage to ask her. I had to do it that night, as I knew I wouldn't rest until I'd done it. So I plucked up the courage to leave my stool and walk over to reception to ask her if she would join me on the trip. I felt like a teenager about to ask for his first date!

I could tell by the way her shoulders sagged and the slight sadness in those beautiful eyes that her answer was going to be no. She said she was taking Saturday off instead of Tuesday as she was going to a festival with her mum, who she said was also her best friend. She did say 'But I want to go with you, I've wanted to go there since I was little'. That made me feel good at least. 'But you are little!' I said. That made her smile. I was disappointed but not downhearted.

I did get a chance for another photograph with her, wearing her new uniform, as did all the reception team. It was a grey tunic dress which was very figure-hugging. She said she didn't find it flattering, but I disagreed – I thought it was very flattering!

I had only been on holiday for two days, but it felt much longer. So much was happening, and all good. Now I had my half-day trip to look forward to.

While I was in the pool, Angus told me Chelsea's birthday was coming up, and I came up with another idea. I was due back at the hotel in August, and I decided to see if I could keep it a secret and surprise both Chelsea and Michela. It would be difficult to surprise Michela of course because she would see my name on the guest list, so I asked Mr Stathis asked if there was any way of coming back without Michela knowing. He said, 'I'll just have to persuade Michela it's not you when she sees your name on the booking list'. We swapped mobile numbers so I could let him know. He warned me not to post anything on Facebook about my holiday. I wrote a daily diary post on Facebook every morning, an idea suggested by my social worker. It started out as rehabilitation news to let everyone know how I was doing, but soon turned into a general diary for all my friends to read. 'Chelsea will be easy, I can keep her out of the way until you arrive,' said Mr Stathis. Her birthday was before my surprise holiday, so I would send a card to the hotel for her. In the meantime my 'angel of the north' continued to rub sun cream into my right arm, totally unaware of my plan!

As my week went on I realised I hadn't done much about my research project, so I decided to talk to my friend Sheri about how she had made the move out to Cyprus, and what she had brought with her. She said that if I rented an apartment in Cyprus it would be fully furnished, so I wouldn't need to bring out any major furniture. She had bought an unfurnished house many years before, so she had moved everything out in a shipping container. These are huge containers which can move the contents of an entire house and even a car – you pay for the amount of space you use. Sheri said I should start making a list of things I wanted or needed to bring with me. My option of moving to Cyprus now seemed to be my first choice, perfect for rebuilding my life and starting a new one. It seemed harsh to start a new life with nothing and nobody to fall back on, but it was the only way if I wanted my independent living. Doing everything again for myself would make stronger, as Michela had told me. If I stayed on in Newcastle I would have the care team dropping in on me for the foreseeable future, and would I progress?

I made a point of going to see Michela the evening before her day out with her mum to wish her a great day out. I could tell by the look in her eyes that this had gone down well. They say the eyes are the gateway to the soul, and if that's true I could see deep into Michela's soul, and it was breathtaking. Michela wished me a good time on my trip to Famagusta. I don't know what would have happened if she had come with me on that trip, how close we would have become. All I know is that I would have treated her as my princess.

I was up early on the day of the trip and packing my backpack. Michela had arranged a packed lunch for me. I would need my passport, as we were going over the border into the Turkish side of the island, or northern Cyprus as it has been known since Turkey invaded in 1974. Anton had arranged a seat for me a few yards behind the driver, so I didn't have to walk far and could stretch out my left leg when I needed to. Famagusta is only just along the coast, so it was a short journey. It took longer by road as you had to pass border control and show your passport. The area was also a big military base.

The passengers all stayed together as a group as our tour guide led us around Famagusta, holding up a big clipboard for us to follow. As on my trip to Nicosia, I don't think anyone noticed my slight hobble, and of course I was even stronger now. I liked what I saw of the walled town, which reminded me of York. The port area reminded me of the old town of Rhodes, one of my favourite places. We had time to ourselves for lunch and a bit of shopping, and I nibbled on the packed lunch Michela had arranged for me. I had heard about the battle-scarred hotels on the seafront of Famagusta, and now I found myself standing in front of them, shell-torn and looking exactly as they had after the battles of 1974. You weren't allowed to take photographs of the shelled hotels, so I didn't. We also weren't allowed to enter the old part of Famagusta, known as the 'ghost town', which is sealed off by the army. It had remained untouched since the town had been evacuated following the invasion. The residents had all fled, leaving everything as it was, right down the clothes on the clothes lines. Even the big open-top bus that takes holidaymakers around on tours doesn't enter.

However the beach at Famagusta looked fabulous, with fine white sand just as you see on pictures of tropical islands, leading down to a beautiful turquoise sea. I found a very nice beachside taverna/restaurant for lunch with splendid views of the beach and the ocean. The people on this side of the island seemed friendly, and I had fun with the staff of the restaurant when I went up to the counter after finding a table. They asked me for my table number and I said 'zero'. They laughed and explained that the 'one' was missing – it was actually table 10.

As I sat eating my tuna salad and a cold drink on this hot day I thought of Michela and wondered how her colour festival was going.

It was nice to have a bit of time to look around the many little shops. I saw a straw hat in one of them, and if Michela had been with me I would have bought it for her, my way of showing her how I would have treated her as my princess. She would have looked lovely in it.

It was soon time to get back to the meeting point and follow the tour guide with the clipboard back to the coach. Although the coach was almost full, the seat next to mine by the window was empty, so I put my pack on it.

I felt that if Turkey hadn't invaded Cyprus in that summer of 1974 the Famagusta of today would probably look very different, more like Monte Carlo, and the resorts of Protaras and Ayia Napa might never have appeared.

Michela had had a good time at the colour festival with her mum. The pictures she posted on Facebook looked fun, and with her face covered in powder paint she looked beautiful and sexy.

Soon I was back on my lounger in my 'office' at the hotel getting a couple of hours relaxing in the sun. I needed to do more research, but I could do that tonight during red wine time, as I planned to take the opportunity to ask Paniyotis about the cost of renting an apartment. He told me I could get one in the Kapparis area for around 250 euros a month. This was another step closer to the move to Cyprus becoming a reality. It was far cheaper than any rent back in the UK and there was no council tax to pay, only 69 euros a month refuse tax to have the bins emptied. In Newcastle I paid £55 a month in council tax and my one-bedroom apartment was £410 a month, although that did include heating and water, a deal done by the St Cuthbert's Court owners.

Now everything was starting to point towards moving to Cyprus. I had got a pension deal sorted out and in a few weeks my divorce would be final, so I would have no ties. It would have been very different if my dad had been alive. I would of course talk to Darren and get his blessing. I would have a lot to do once I got back home, but I was looking forward to that, as knowing I would be making a surprise return shortly would make leaving less of a heartache!

When I got home I learned that Tablet Woman was leaving the pharmacy to work for a cleaning company, so she would not be delivering my medication any more. On the face of it this was devastating news, but it was another push in the direction of a move to Cyprus. In fact I was beginning to tell people around me of my plans. Those close to me, such as Wendy and Margaret at St Cuthbert's and Joanie and Den at the café across the road, didn't seem surprised to hear my plans.

During my Tuesday evening visit to Simply Greek I had a conversation with Dimitri and Anna and we discussed the transportation of my possessions. They explained how the shipping containers worked. You paid by the cubic metre for the amount of space you used. They told me how wonderful my idea sounded, which was the first time anyone had said that. They also said they were envious of me, but they wouldn't have said that if they had appreciated what I had been through to get to this stage of my life.

I was excited about going to Lisa at Thomas Cook again about my plan for a surprise trip to Cyprus. I asked her if there was anything she could do to help me to keep it secret, and she said it might be possible if we booked the flight and the hotel separately. This would mean I would have to make my own arrangements for the transfer to the hotel. I told her to book everything. I still had to pay for the additional medical travel insurance and go through the medical screening questions, but my payments were much lower now because of my progress.

I sent a birthday card to Chelsea at the hotel and bought her a watch for her birthday, and for Michela I bought a box of chocolates, a cuddly toy and a card with a matching teddy on the front.

It felt strange not to write anything on my daily Facebook page about my forthcoming trip. I did let Mr Stathis and Angus know by text, but they were the only people in Cyprus who knew.

I promised myself I would do more research during my surprise week. I needed to check if I could get all the medication I needed out there, and how and where from.

If I couldn't do this then my move would be a non-starter. I reasoned that it must be possible, as there were so many ex-pats from the UK living there. I knew of two pharmacies near the hotel and decided to ask them. I knew I would have to pay for medication in Cyprus, of course. It seemed that the more questions I asked myself, the fewer answers I got. Everything seemed so difficult. This wasn't just about the lure of the blue skies, the blue Mediterranean, the red wine and the beauty of Michela – it was everything else I had to think about. I had to get this decision right!

It was soon time for me to be sitting in the departure lounge again at Newcastle Airport waiting for a gate number for Flight TCX6108 to Larnaca. I liked these early starts – I've always loved the mornings, even as a kid growing up and doing a paper round. At John Lewis I enjoyed the early morning starts, part of a rota I'd had great pleasure in creating.

I caught sight of Gemma at the top of the aircraft steps, standing and welcoming passengers and checking their boarding passes. I have been told this is the cabin crew's least favourite duty. She took my hand luggage and escorted me to my seat. It felt good to be given such treatment by someone so beautiful. She asked why I was making such a quick return to Cyprus, joking that I was flying there more often than some of her colleagues! I explained my plans as she knelt beside me. By the look in her gorgeous eyes I thought she was going to say she wanted to come with me

– that would have put the cat among the pigeons! 'Oh how I would love to do that, living the dream,' she said, so again someone was feeling envious of my plan.

Landing at Larnaca was different this time, as after passing security and coming out into the arrivals hall, instead of looking for the Thomas Cook rep I had to look for my name being held up by one of the taxi firms. I can tell you it felt cool to see my name on a board! I was soon in a taxi and on my way to the hotel, ahead of all the coaches. I sent Mr Stathis a text to say I had landed, and he replied that he would be waiting in the lobby. He would also text Chelsea to meet him there. No doubt wondering if she had something wrong, she made her way to the lobby from the pool area, where she had been busy with the daytime entertainments programme.

The timing was perfect – it couldn't have gone any better. I arrived in the lobby just as Chelsea got there, and tears started to roll down her face. I was shocked at this reaction, and Mr Stathis asked her why she was crying. Before I knew it she had flung herself into my arms. I didn't get this sort of thing in the UK! Then, just as it couldn't have got any better, Michela came over from the desk, looking more stunningly beautiful than ever. She seemed smaller – or was it that I was standing taller these days, back to my original height of six feet?

'I knew you were coming,' she said. 'I saw your name on the room list and knew it was you.' She then said she was going to give me a different room, as I had been given one on the mezzanine floor, between the ground lobby area and the first floor, and these rooms didn't have much of a view. Now she knew it was me, she was going to give me a room on the third floor as usual, with wonderful views of the sea. But what a welcome! The memory will stay with me for ever. Moments like that don't come around very often, if ever! My plan had worked out perfectly.

After unpacking it was time to deliver the gifts to my girls. First down to reception to see Michela. There was a different look this time in her eyes, one I couldn't explain as I had never seen it before. Our eyes met in a gaze that neither of us could break away from. She said she liked the fact that I had tried to surprise her. She had asked Mr Stathis if the booking was me, but he had denied it. 'I like it that you tried to surprise me,' she said. 'I like surprises, what girl doesn't? I also like what you did for Chelsea, it was sweet.' All my planning and hard work had paid off – it had worked out better than I had ever imagined.

Next I went to see Chelsea, who was busy with the daytime entertainment activities. I gave her the watch and the little bag of chocolates and there were more tears and hugs. Unknown to me Paniyotis had been watching all this, and I had a laugh later at the bar when he asked me 'So where's my gift and my chocolates?'

It was a great start to my surprise holiday, and it got even better with more progress in the pool and also in the sea. Angus and Chelsea kept me steady as I walked down the beach and into the sea, as I hadn't walked on sand since before my stroke. Once again Mr Stathis was supervising everything in his shirt and tie amidst all the holidaymakers on their loungers and towels. This time there was going to be photographic evidence of what I was achieving with him in charge of my camera, taking pictures which Angus would download onto my tablet so I could put them on my Facebook page for all my friends to see what was happening and how well I was doing. I think Mr Stathis was enjoying doing this as it got him out of his office! He also enjoyed being outside chatting to the guests as they soaked up the sun.

It felt so very good to be in the sea. I had often been in the sea before my stroke, although I was not a strong swimmer. It's part of life in the Greek islands, and it's fun! I have often played bat and ball with girls in the sea. I could feel myself being lifted and pushed about by the waves as I stood on the sandy sea bottom. This could only help my balance and make me feel stronger. I was enjoying myself and wanted to stay in the water, but I knew I was taking up too much of Angus and Chelsea's time, even if they were happy to go on.

It was time to look into the most critical issue I needed to research, how to get my medication if I moved over here. I decided to visit a pharmacy with a list of all the medication

I was taking. Chelsea came with me, out of interest and to give me some support if needed. Result! Everything I was taking was available here. This was a big step forward, and it was cause for a small celebration during red wine time that evening.

That week Michela got some help in reception from a new girl, Maria, who was just as beautiful and even more sexy, and had a mischievous glint in her eyes. She looked Greek or Cypriot with her dark hair and eyes, so I tried some of my Greek on her. 'This is not my country' she replied. It turned out that she was from Bulgaria. She would work different shifts each day, working alongside Michela on the busy afternoon shift.

I had noticed how much more fluent my Greek was getting and how much faster I could respond when spoken to. It was helped by my daily banter with Slavi, the maintenance man, to whom I gave the nickname 'megalos gharos', meaning 'big donkey'. It was all in fun and taken that way. It was also good to have daily conversations with Mr Stathis at a table outside. I still had to convince Michela, my taskmaster, who still formulated a sentence for me to say to her in Greek each day. If I got it wrong, she would send me away to work out how to get it right! Maria found this very amusing. The advantage of having them both on the afternoon shift was that on karaoke evenings Michela could come and stand on the balcony above the stage to hear me sing 'What a Wonderful World' while Maria looked after reception. Once again that week the song went well, and many people came onto the balcony to listen.

Chapter 9

In at the deep end

Although I was on an all-inclusive package, I didn't always have lunch at the hotel. Sometimes I would go for a quiet stroll along the boardwalk which ran past the hotel along the coast, as it got me off my lounger. I felt I could do this now even in the heat of the day. I would stop off for a cold drink and a snack in one of the kiosks along the way. I think the boardwalk ran all the way to the next resort, Penera, which would make a lovely scenic walk.

During one of these strolls I stopped to read a board and some leaflets with information about a boat trip. The man sitting at the table asked me if I was interested, and I told him I was, but wasn't sure if I could get on the boat. He looked at me and said 'You have to believe you can do it'. He was the captain of the boat, and told me it did two-hour trips along the coast. 'I believe you can do it,' he added. I had mastered so many forms of transport during my recovery – planes, trains, buses, coaches and trams – and getting on a boat would be really something, the last one to conquer. And a day on the water in a boat would be good for the tan! So I paid my 10 euros and the captain explained where the boat would depart from, a small wooden jetty which was about a 15-minute walk from the hotel. He said I should get there in plenty of time for the 11 am departure so he could help me onto the boat and look after me on the two-and-a-half-hour trip. He told me he had to leave on time as he had another booking for 1 pm.

I wondered what the 'what if' people back home would have made of this, and spent the rest of the afternoon relaxing on my lounger in readiness for what I thought might be a tough day tomorrow. I got a lot of support and 'good for yous' from my wonderful friends at the hotel during red wine time.

On the morning of the trip I made sure I had a substantial cooked English breakfast instead of my normal yoghurt, fruit and honey, as I had a good walk to and from the boat and the time I would be spending at sea. I was glad I had, as it was hot morning and the walk along the boardwalk was a tough one carrying my backpack, which was packed with my towel, a book, sun cream and a bottle of water. The captain was waiting at the jetty, which looked a small pier and was quite high above the water. That meant steps, and there were plenty of them, metal ones, eroded by sea water and sea breezes. The captain told me to follow him down the steps and take my time. We stopped about two steps from the bottom, and from there he jumped into the boat. 'You can do this,' he assured me. I took another step down and braced myself. 'I'll catch you' he assured me. I could feel his belief in me, which gave me more confidence. I looked around to see a long line of other passengers coming down the steps and could almost hear their groans of impatience, but I didn't care what they thought of me. I just took a huge leap, as it seemed to me, and landed safely next to the captain. I was on the boat! I felt like celebrating my latest and greatest achievement so far.

The next thing was to get used to standing and walking on the boat while out at sea with the constant motion of the boat on the water. It's hard enough with two good legs, so this was going to be one test I couldn't celebrate passing just yet.

I took a seat at the back of the boat and we were under way. The trip took us along the coast to the border with Turkey. The captain was not allowed to cross into Turkish waters – stupid really, as it's all the same sea. We had to stop at a point marked by buoys, from which you could see the hotels of Famagusta, the same ones I had seen during my previous holiday. It was a good chance for those with decent cameras to take pictures. I have never seen the sea as blue as it was there on that day. It looked as if a giant tub of royal blue paint had been poured into it. It was very hot now, so I was glad I was wearing my cap.

After we had turned round we sailed back along the coast, past our hotel and the beaches to a rocky cove called Cape Grecco. Here there are the chance to jump into the sea for a swim, and most of the passengers took this opportunity. As the boat emptied I took the opportunity to walk down to a desk selling cold drinks and snacks and buy a drink and a ham and cheese cob. I could have gone without both, but the main reason for going down there was to see if I could walk along the boat while we were out at sea with the motion of the waves. I had no trouble! I was glad I had done this while the boat was empty, because when the other passengers all piled back on board the boat started to get very wet.

After this stop we headed back to our jetty, passing paragliders being pulled by speedboats. I wondered if I should put that on my bucket list! The next challenge was climbing out of the boat and up the steps. The captain again offered his help, but I knew this was going to be more difficult. I took a big step up and almost fell, taking the captain with me, but I didn't. I thanked him for his help and made my way back up the iron steps for the stroll back to the hotel. It felt a lot longer than it had in the morning as my legs were feeling heavy now, but at least by taking the early trip I now had some time to relax on my lounger before red wine time.

It wasn't until later that evening, during red wine time, that I realised something odd – on the boat nobody had asked me what was wrong with me or what had happened to me. Not that I was looking for sympathy, but I had got so used to being asked questions about it that I had come to expect it. Now that it wasn't happening any more, it took me by surprise. It seemed that the only logical step now was indeed for me to move to Cyprus as planned. It had already been decided that Kapparis would be the ideal place for me to live, and Sheri was going to look for a suitable apartment for me. By the time I came to Cyprus in October I might even be able to start viewing suitable places.

I knew that when I got home I would have a lot to do. Although I never liked leaving Cyprus, I was looking forward to getting on with the arrangements for my new life. It had been a brilliant week as so much had happened, and once again I felt so much better and stronger as a person. I also felt I had become closer to both Chelsea and Michela after my surprise arrival. I will never forget that moment and the response I got from them, and I don't think they will either.

There was a strange look in Michela's eyes as I said goodbye to her that Monday evening, the same look I had noticed all week. It was a difficult goodbye with Chelsea too on the Wednesday morning, but that wasn't the last I saw of her, as she came running towards me as I waited for my taxi transfer to the airport to give me one last huge hug.

As I was in a taxi, I arrived at the airport ahead of all the coaches, so there were no queues to check in. As I sat having a drink and a snack in the airport bar after passing security, I could see something was happening at the table in front of me. A young girl from Saudi Arabia was a short of what she needed to pay her bill. The bar assistant wasn't going to let her off and the girl was starting to panic as she was afraid of missing her flight to Riyadh. I stepped in to supply the one euro she needed and she was able to pay her bill and catch her flight.

Back in Newcastle, I got cracking. From Dimitri and Anna I had got the email addresses of several shipping companies and wrote to them about my plan, with a list of items. The replies I got soon told me this wasn't going to work, as the minimum space you could book was far more than I needed – my stuff would have fitted in the back of a van. Dimitri and Anna were not entirely surprised. Maybe I should start again and simply leave everything behind, which was what my friends Viv and Pete from near Mansfield suggested. After all, you can replace clothes and books, and I wouldn't need my warm clothes for the English winter. I decided to leave this question open for now.

I also had a couple more meetings at work. It was

agreed that I would take retirement from the age of 48 through ill health and retire on a monthly ill-health pension with a small lump sum which would be enough to get me to Cyprus and help set everything up. The details were agreed, and all I had to do was sign all the paperwork. I would be retiring 17 years early, and I felt I certainly had 17 years of work left in me.

Next I headed to the bank, HSBC on Gosforth High Street, for a meeting with the branch service manager. I wanted to keep the account I had with them, as they were a huge bank with branches around the world. The meeting caused some confusion, as all I wanted to do was tell them I was planning to move to Cyprus and ask if I could keep my account going as I didn't want any complications. The service manager wanted my new address on Cyprus, which of course I didn't have yet. This reminded me that I had to get back out there to find a place, and this meant another trip to see Lisa at Thomas Cook.

The bank assured me I could keep my account with them, although there was no branch in Cyprus – I just had to give them all my new details before I left. I was told to come back and arrange another meeting with the customer service manager. I was hoping I would be able to do this after my October visit.

To see Lisa I made a point of mixing up my transport, getting the Metro from near my home, then walking to the travel agency. 'I want to go back,' I said, and told her I wanted a week in early October. I had a coffee with her as she printed off my details. I was now a VIP customer, so I got a good rate on my euros from the exchange desk.

On September 11, my lump sum and my first pension payment appeared in my bank account. I could now do some clothes shopping. I also remembered that on my last trip Maria had asked me to bring her an octopus (not a real one, obviously). Was it a bit of flirting? I wasn't sure what Michela would make of it. I didn't want to let Maria down, so I went in search of an octopus toy, without much success. I got my carer involved in one of my shopping trips – it was not Lennon now but David, and he spotted a rubber toy squid that came free with a bottle of soap. That was near enough, I thought, and I felt sure Maria would appreciate the effort I had made to find it. If it made her smile, it was job done for me! I would find out what she thought very soon.

My lovely friend Sheri said she might have found an apartment in the Kapparis area for me. She had arranged for me to meet a contact called Linzie at a rental office there called Buy Let Cyprus, to discuss my requirements. I wanted my holiday to start now and not have to wait for weeks!

With this news I knew it was time to start the all-too-familiar chocolate and gift shop. I bought Maria some chocolates as well, just in case she felt left out when the presents were handed round!

Soon it was time for the return trip, and once again there was Gemma waiting for me with her friendly smile. As the crew walked through towards the plane it occurred to me that the wheeled cases they were pulling behind them made the men look slightly gay, and that made me wonder what I looked like myself when I was pulling my cabin bag. As usual Gemma did the coffee run and helped me with the little containers. I told her my plans were going well and I was hoping to view an apartment or two during my visit 'Oh how exciting, I look forward to hearing about it next week,' she said. She had asked to do the Larnaca run all summer, so she would be on board for my return next week. She leaned over to serve the other two passengers in my row and as always, she smelt so good.

On my arrival at the hotel Michela and Mr Stathis were waiting for me, and it was Michela who checked me in. After unpacking, it was as usual time for me to deliver my gifts. Michela was in reception, and when our eyes met I felt the usual electricity between us. Maria was there too, working the afternoon shift with her, so I gave her the toy squid. She looked so happy to receive it and the chocolates, and both girls laughed cheekily as they opened the chocolates and tasted them. I had to get a photograph of Maria's beautiful happy smile as she held the squid – nice that such a small thing can make someone so happy.

Mr Stathis then led me and Maria away to take our photo, and made us hold hands. Only after he had done it did I realise that he had put us under the 'Just Married' sign in the area where weddings were advertised!

Speaking to Sheri later, she told me she had arranged for me to meet Linzie from the Buy Let Cyprus office to view an apartment on Friday.

During red wine time that evening I spoke to Michela and Maria to check that they were both OK with the picture Mr Stathis had taken under the 'Just Married' sign. Everybody was fine with it, so I was free to enjoy my wine and get into the zone for karaoke performance later – Chelsea and Angus had arranged it for that night. With Maria there, Michela could again come out and watch from the balcony. I could have done with an early night after my day of travelling, but my performance went well and Michela again scored me 12 out of 10.

I was looking forward to relaxing in the hot October sun the next day, before my busy day on Friday. Sheri said she would take me to the agency office on her way home from her morning shift, so I agreed to be in reception at 12.45. I thought about this as I had coffee on my balcony. Today I could be seeing my new home for the first time.

My first impression of Kapparis was that I liked it. It looked like many of the tourist areas you find on any Greek island. Linzie was very welcoming and bubbly and we got on fine as we walked down the avenue to the one-bedroomed apartment at no 78 Sunny Coast, which had a small outdoor area with a patio table and sun lounger. The sea was about a five-minute walk away across watermelon fields. We went back into the office to discuss a date for taking on the apartment if I wanted it. I remember Michela telling me spring was a nice time of year in Cyprus, and moving then would let me get used to the climate progressively before the heat of the summer. Mr Stathis had also told me I should visit in the winter to see it on a cold and cloudy day. I had been thinking of coming in December to see the apartment, with a view to moving in March 2016. I paid Linzie a deposit of 250 euros to secure a second viewing, and after we had had a drink in the Kennedy pub opposite her office, she gave me a lift back to the hotel. This pub would be my local if I moved there. I liked Linzie, who said she was from Lichfield in Staffordshire, and wanted to be a singer. She also worked at the Lazy Frog pub in Protaras, which we passed on the way back to the hotel.

I was looking forward to telling my friends about my day, and the first one I told was Sheri when she opened the shop at 5pm. She was delighted to hear I had liked the apartment. Next was Michela as I passed reception at red wine time, and the look in her gorgeous hazel eyes told me everything as I told my princess about my day. It was the perfect time for a photograph together, and Mr Andreas took one. My wine was waiting for me when I got to the bar, and I had a drink with Mr Stathis to tell him about the apartment. He joined me for dinner, and he told me it was a good idea to come out in December to see it in winter, although of course it had been his idea.

On the Saturday I made sure I had a full day on the lounger in my 'office' – after all this was supposed to be a holiday – and Chelsea, my angel of the north, rubbed the oil on my right arm as usual. But Saturday soon turned into Monday and before I knew it, it was time to say goodbye to Michela again. It would be a difficult goodbye as always, but I was looking forward to getting home as I had plenty to do getting the December holiday booked – Michela told me I would have to use an on-line company called Mercury Direct. I also wanted to go to Nottingham to tell my brother about my plans.

As I was waiting in the lobby for my 11 am coach to the airport, something happened that took me completely by surprise. Maria, who was on the morning shift, walked slowly over to me, put her arms around me and gave me a hug that was full of warmth and love, the kind of hug you'd only expect from a loved one. The look on Anton's face was a picture – it had surprised him too. He was waiting for a coach from his tour company to take a group of holidaymakers to the airport. As I boarded the coach I could think of nothing else but that wonderful hug. The transfer seemed much faster than usual, in fact the whole journey went quickly and I was soon back in my flat at St Cuthbert's Court.

On my next trip into Newcastle I went into Thomas Cook to tell Lisa about my plan to move to Cyprus, as she had been a big part of my adventure. She was excited for me and wanted to be kept updated. When I told her I would have to go via Mercury Direct, I was surprised and delighted to hear her say, 'No you don't, I can sort that out for you.' She explained that Thomas Cook acted as a 'silent agent' for Mercury Direct and could book holidays and flights for them. She said that if I dropped in one day she would sort it all out for me, and I told her I was off to Nottingham but I would call in on my return. This called for a celebratory red wine at the Mezze bar!

Soon after this I was packing my bags for my midweek trip to Nottingham. I now knew this journey so well that I found it easy, but I still always got on board early to claim a seat on the right so I could stretch my left leg out.

When I saw my brother and explained my plans, he invited me to stay with the family at Christmas again, as it might be the last opportunity for some time. That made me decide to return to Cyprus earlier in the month. We spent time on his computer looking at the Buy Let Cyprus website and they were showing a photograph of no 78 Sunny Coast, even though I had paid a deposit to reserve it. They all liked what they saw, and it felt good to get my brother's blessing for my plans.

One evening I went to see my Greek friend Emilo at his restaurant. Over a lovely dinner we discussed my plans and I mentioned the problem of getting my belongings to Cyprus. He said he might be able to help and surprised me by telling me he had friends in Paralimni.

As arranged, once home I went back to see Lisa to arrange the holiday. She was wonderful and managed to make all the arrangements. There were no flights from Newcastle to Larnaca so I would have to fly from Manchester Airport to Paphos on the other side of the island, which would mean an overnight stay at Manchester Airport. Lisa booked everything for me, including the transfer from Newcastle to Manchester Airport and back, stating at the Crown Plaza. There would be a two-and-a-half-hour taxi ride from Paphos to Protaras, which Lisa also sorted. The whole journey as going to take two days each way, the first day going by train to Manchester Airport and the second from there to Protaras. It would be a very big test of my strength and staying power, especially as I would have to change trains at York both ways with my suitcase and hand luggage, and the possibility of bad weather. But I was looking forward to the challenge.

I left the agency without any paperwork, as Lisa suggested it would be better to come back and pick everything up when she had everything, including the rail tickets and my hotel documents. Lisa had again been wonderful sorting everything out for me, so when I left the agency I went to a barrow-boy's stall and bought her a nice bunch of flowers. She was surprised to see what I had done, but I could tell she was pleased. Once again I popped into Mezze for a glass of red wine and sat watching everyone going about their business. I started thinking about a date for my move, and remembering what Michela had said about January and February being the worst two months of the year, I decided that March 1 would be a good date. This was only provisional, but it would be good to have a date to work to.

A few days later I had a call from Lisa to say that my documents were all waiting for me, and went once again into Newcastle to collect them.

Now I had to let Michela know and contact Buy Let Cyprus to tell them I wanted to view the apartment again. This was going to be much more than a holiday, and it would be very different from the summer weeks spent on my lounger and in the bar. Chelsea and Angus would not be there as the entertainment team was not needed in the winter, and Anton would not be at work. In fact the hotel was very popular in the winter, even though the resort virtually closed down. It would be interesting to see what Protaras was like when it wasn't full of tourists. At least Michela would still be in reception and Paniyotis would still be in the bar. Although I wanted to see what Cyprus was like in the winter, I hoped it would still be sunny enough for me to lie on my lounger. Of course I still had to work out what items I would be taking with me and how I was going to get them there, but I was hoping Emilo would be able to help me here.

It was a cold, misty December morning when I left Newcastle station on the Trans-Pennine express to York with its attractive green and purple livery. Most of my fellow passengers were dressed in jumpers and big winter coats, while I was wearing a T-shirt under my fleece as I was travelling to a warmer climate. I had chosen an early morning train to give myself plenty of time to change at York. I had all day to get to the hotel at Manchester Airport.

A trolley service was available, so I was able to have a coffee brought to my seat. I had my medication in my hand luggage, so I could take my lunchtime tablet with a sandwich and a drink at York station.

As we approached York I could see a few pockets of snow on the ground, and it felt cold as I waited to change trains. There were lifts between the platforms, but I still found it difficult to manage with my trolley case and hand luggage to carry. The train to Manchester Airport was going from Platform 13, and I noticed that it was the only train that used it. It was obviously a popular service, as there was a café there, which gave me a chance to sit down and have a coffee and a bacon sandwich. While I ate my snack I reflect that I could never have been doing this a year ago.

My plan was to check in at the hotel after 3 pm and then have a leisurely red wine at the bar before eating in the restaurant, followed by more red wine time later. I had Facebook on my Nokia phone and kept in contact with Michela throughout my journey. I guessed my arrival time would not be until after 11 pm, the time she finished, so I would not see her until the day after. She had said she had thought of working till midnight, but I told her not to as her shift was quite long enough as it was.

When we got to the station at Manchester Airport, most of my fellow passengers headed off towards the terminal while I went to find the bus stop for the airport shuttle to the Crown Plaza. I had to dial a freephone number, and I was answered with a voice addressing me by name and telling me a shuttle was on its way. Fifteen minutes later a minibus arrived to take me to the hotel.

The five-hour flight with Easy Jet went fine, as did the two-and-a-half hour drive to the Constantinos the Great Hotel. I arrived just before midnight to find that Michela had allocated room 325 to me, a fabulous room on the third floor overlooking the pool and the ocean. When I woke up on my first morning, it was hard to believe that we were in December. There was a perfect clear blue sky as I had coffee on my balcony and listened to the little birds singing away. The glassy calm ocean looked just as it had on my other visits. I was so looking forward to seeing Michela's gorgeous smile.

After breakfast at the usual table I decided to take a stroll around the hotel to see which of my many friends on the staff were on duty. A few had gone home to their own countries and families for the winter, but most of them were there, which made everything feel fine. Among them was Maria, who now lived in Cyprus. I had a small bag of chocolates for her, as I did for Michela. I thought I would wait until Michela started work before handing them out. I had other things to do though in connection with my move plans. I called Buy Let Cyprus to let them know I had arrived and arranged another viewing of no. 78 Sunny Coast. I was rather shocked to find that Linzie had now left the agency to pursue her dream of becoming a singer, starting at the Lazy Frog pub with a live spot on a Friday evening. My folder had been handed over to a new girl called Fiona, and I arranged to meet her in a couple of days, to give the chance to spend some time resting on my lounger.

I did get some time in my 'office' on my lounger, but I felt restless and kept looking at the time, wanting the clock to move on to 3 pm so I could make my way up to reception to see Michela. It did feel good to be on my lounger though. It was a warm day at 22 degrees with a cloudless blue sky, and to my surprise the Sea Breeze kiosk was serving cold drinks, snacks and coffee. I heard that Mr Stathis had decided to open it as the hotel was full. Strangely though, it was playing Christmas songs! It felt strange listening to them while lying basking in warm sunshine.

Finally it was time to go down to reception and be treated to Michela's beautiful warm smile. A large decorated Christmas tree stood there – it was hard to believe that Christmas was only 20 days away! I gave

Michela her teddy and chocolates, along with a card, and gave Maria her chocolates too. Paniyotis had seen all this and once again joked, 'More gifts! Where's mine?'

I think Michela liked my choice of cuddly toy more than usual, as she gave me a lovely mischievous look. This time it was one from the Boofle range. It had its hands over its eyes, with the words 'When I do this I can pretend you're not very far away XXX'. Cute, I thought, as I missed her so much every time I left Cyprus. I believed this told her I missed her, along with the card, if she didn't know already.

As part of my research, Mr Stathis had kindly arranged for me to meet some of his friends so they could tell me about life on Cyprus. I would miss my evening dinner, as I would be joining them to go to a traditional taverna in the village of Sotira for a traditional mezze meal. I saw that there were no menus on the table – everyone was ordering without them, and the food and wine kept coming. They seemed a great set of lads, and the six of us got on really well, although afterwards I couldn't remember any of their names. Outside I could see a large Christmas tree all lit up with the Greek words for 'Happy Christmas'. I learned from them the saying 'You don't drink wine until it's time', a catchy slogan which I still use now. They also advised me that I should always keep wine in the apartment and cold beer in the fridge.

I learned that to have a good life in Cyprus I would need an income of only around 800 euros a month, which was good to know. With my pension and the money I had in my bank account I wouldn't be too far short of that.

It was late when Mr Stathis drove me back to the hotel, but I was still up early the next morning to have coffee on my balcony before breakfast at 7, so I could listen to the birdsong and look out over the blue Mediterranean. I would have the morning to myself until 11, when Fiona from Buy Let Cyprus would pick me up for my second viewing of the flat in Kapparis.

Fiona duly picked me up and drove me to the office, where Carolyn had some news for me. She said another apartment had become available on the same block, no. 81, which had a much bigger outdoor space. That was what I wanted, as I planned to spend most of my time out of doors. I agreed to have a look, and we walked down the avenue to view it. It did indeed have a wonderful large patio, big enough for a full-size table, four chairs and two sun loungers with space to spare. I liked it, but I still wanted to have another look at no. 78. It seemed a lot smaller now, and no. 81 was south facing, so I would get the sun all day.

We went back to the office to agree terms for no. 81. My earlier payment of 250 euros would secure the property and the rent was the same as no. 78 at 250 euros a month, so I would just to find the first month's rent. The apartment would be mine from March 1st. If I decided not to make the move I would of course lose my 500 euros.

With all the paperwork signed, Fiona gave me a lift

back to the Constantinos in plenty of time for me to tell Michela about my day when she started her shift at 3 pm. I had taken a big step forward towards moving to Cyprus and leaving behind my care package and the safety net of the ERD scheme. There would be no one to fall back on – I would have to look after myself full time. I knew it would be difficult to convince the professionals responsible for my care that it was the right thing to do, but it was my life and this was the best way for me to make it a good one.

Then there was more good news: my friend Emilo got in touch to say that he had found a solution to the problem of getting my belongings to Cyprus. A Greek company called Mondial had a lorry that went from London to Limassol one day a week. This would be the perfect solution. I would have to ring them, as their business was done over the phone. I arranged to see Emilo at his restaurant in Nottingham at Christmas to get the details.

When I told Michela about my day, she seemed genuinely pleased for me. I could see happiness in her beautiful eyes as she assured me 'It will be a better life for you in Cyprus, you will make a good Cypriot'. Michela was always right!

She agreed that on her day off on Tuesday we would have a coffee together at Costa Coffee. It was going to be a truly red wine time tonight! I hadn't even realised there was a Costa Coffee in Protaras. I spent most of the evening looking over to reception from my stool at the bar to watch her at work. Michela didn't just walk – she would glide.

On the Tuesday I was at Costa Coffee early to wait for my princess. What a lovely setting it was, with a raised wooden decking area giving wonderful views over the blue ocean. The decking area had nice wicker seating and matching tables. Michela wanted to sit inside by the electric fire, where it was warmer, but I wanted to be outside in the sun. We sat inside! Two years earlier my world had come crashing down on me, but she had shown me what a wonderful world I still had around me. She had changed my life without doing anything except be herself, from the moment I first saw her everlasting smile of warmth and beauty. Now I was about to begin a new life and start a new story.

I looked at Michela. She looked so beautiful in her boots, jeans and white jumper, duffle coat and white woolly hat, as if she had just stepped out of a fashion catalogue photoshoot, while I was in sandals, shorts and T-shirt. It must have been around 18 degrees outside.

Suddenly she said to me, 'Why are you laughing at me?' I replied, 'I'm not, but there you are all wrapped up while I'm in my shorts and T-shirt!'

'But it's cold!' she said.

I told her she should be living in England, where it really did get cold. She looked at me with her gorgeous hazel-brown eyes and said, 'Wait until you are living here', then flashed me that amazing smile. I was transfixed by her gaze, and the deal was done. If ever a smile could clinch a deal it was that one. I was moving to Cyprus – and soon!